Tiny and Bubba Go To Town

By Art Fuller

PREFACE

'Going to town' is not exclusively a 'Southern' thing but yet it is in some respects. I don't hear people in the Northeast talk about, 'Well, i reckon I'll go to town tomorrow.' No, they already live in town. So, why would they need to *go* there?

Tiny and Bubba have recounted to me how they used to 'go to town' with their dads and even grandpas on most Saturday mornings. There was a sawdust field on the edge of town called the Jockey Lot where men went to buy, sell or trade almost anything.

Got a calf you want to get rid of? Take it to the Jockey Lot. Somebody there will give you something for it. Want a new hunting knife or rifle? Somebody will have one at the Jockey Lot. Want to buy a baby goat for your kid (no pun intended)? You knew where you could find one on a Saturday morning…

This place was kind of a precursor to today's Flea Market (Tag Sale if you're up North or swap meet if you're out west). Stuff was sold for its real price (what somebody would actually pay) as opposed to what was advertised in the stores.

Both of the fellas said usually their grandpa would let grandma out on the square in the middle of town (She had shopping to do too!) and then pick her up a couple hours later after making the rounds at the Jockey Lot. So, going to town was a big deal for everybody in the family.

Of course the phrase 'going to town' has another metaphorical meaning as in *really going at something*. For instance, it would be totally appropriate to say, "He's really going to town on that plate of beans and taters!" We Southerners would know exactly what you meant. That's a colloquialism (A big fancy word for *slang* or everyday talk) that resonates with us.

Whatever your memories of going to town are, Tiny and Bubba hope you recall, relive and revive them as they take you through, *Tiny and Bubba Go To Town*.

DEDICATION

Linda Irene continues to laugh at my jokes and stories. By now she's heard so many, it's hard to find a new ones to try out on her. But, I continue to seek out anecdotes that will make her chuckle, giggle or guffaw. After 30 years together that laugh is still one of the most treasured sounds I hear from her.

Keep on laughing, baby!

Additional copies of this book can be ordered at amazon.com. Just search for Tiny and Bubba by Art Fuller.

Be sure to follow Art's author page on Amazon and give this book a 4 or 5 star rating. Tiny and Bubba would appreciate it, y'all!

Appendix - Tiny and Bubba's Family Tree

Family Trees

Some folks have asked to see a listing of Tiny and Bubba's friends, relatives, in-laws and outlaws. I talked with the boys and they said it would be okay to share their hillbilly genetics.

BUBBA'S TREE of Relationships

Boudreaux - Bubba's favorite brother-in-law. Lives in Louisiana with Bubba's sister, Marie. Known to visit big city churches to see what's going on.

Marie - Bubba's sister. Married to Boudreaux. Loves alligator shoes. She and Boudreaux have three children - Thibodeaux, Hebert and Joleene.

Daisy - Bubba's mom. Married to Bubba's dad, Lum. Daughter of Bubba Sr.

Lum - Bubba's dad. Married to his mom, Daisy. Occasionally people get their names confused and refer to them as Dumb and Lazy... Lum's brother's name is Lon.

Bubba Sr. - Bubba's grandpa, father of Daisy, Bubba's mom. Currently retired but formerly a preacher who visited the Holy Land.

Marg - Bubba's best gal. She has a small dog named Roscoe. Frequently on a diet.

AnnaMae - Marg's blonde cousin who spent a short time in a mental institution but now works at a clothing store and occasionally at the DriveRite Truck Stop.

Fred - Bubba's Uncle on his mom's side. Known to tug on a cork on occasion; A habitual jug-tugger.

Evelyn - Bubba's aunt. Married to Uncle Fred. Tolerates his drinking but wants to get him in church.

DelMar (or occasionally spelled Del-mar depending on if he's trying to impress somebody or not) - Bubba's cousin on his dad's side. Graduated from Georgia Tech with an Engineering degree. 1st person in the family to ever attend college. Married / divorced Trudy.

Junior - Bubba's cousin on his mom's side. Helped Bubba put up the new flagpole at the school. Was recently married and divorced after his wife ran off with his pickup truck and his best friend.

Earl - Junior's brother. Lives in Florida and has an alligator pond. Occasionally runs around with his best friend, Bobby.

Sadie - Daisy's sister, oldest daughter of Bubba Sr.

***

TINY'S TREE of Relationships

Mavis Jean - Tiny's sister. She has two *young* adult children, Suzie and Troy Allen.

Suzie - Tiny's niece who works occasionally at the Hair Salon, loves fried chicken and was a handful growing up. Just ask her teachers.

Troy Allen - Tiny's nephew. Tried out for football team at Florida State, has worked for the county highway department in various jobs. Currently looking for work in an office position.

Francine - Tiny's blonde cousin. Works for the Texas Highway Patrol. Married to Charles Thomas.

Charles Thomas - Francine's husband. Plays golf. Adopted a Japanese baby boy with Francine. Fascinated by small things like cribs.

Tizzie - Tiny's aunt. Has a cat named Slug. Married to Merle. Lives next door to an atheist neighbor.

Merle - Tiny's uncle. Truck driver. Married to Tizzie. Also known to tip the moonshine jug on occasion.

Cledy - Tiny's grandma on his dad's side. Has two sons, Cletus and Wade. Had her husband, Homer, cremated. Recently pre-paid her final expenses at the funeral home.

Herschel - Cousin-in-law Charles Thomas's dad. Loves to dispense wisdom about such things as marriage and how to deal with the opposite sex. Not too handy with chainsaws.

Homer - Celery's husband, now deceased. He was in the Air Force after the big war and served pumping sewage out of airplanes in Greenland.

Duh...

Chapter 1 - Going To Town

Drumming Up Some Business

Bubba said his cousin Del-mar has decided to become a lawyer. He's already a Georgia Tech-trained Engineer; Proudly the first member of the family to attend college. (He was mighty disappointed when none of the railroads around would let him drive one of their trains.)

Anyway, with Valentine's Day approaching Bubba was over at Del-mar's house. When he arrived, Del-mar was in the kitchen. There was a stack of Valentine cards on the table and Del-mar was methodically licking a "Love" stamp, putting it on a bright pink envelope and spraying a little perfume on each one.

Bubba asked him, "Del-mar, what in the world are you doing?"

Del-mar smiled a sly grin. "I'm sending out 1,000 Valentine cards signed, 'Guess who?'"

Bubba shook his head and asked, "Why?"

"I'm gonna be a divorce lawyer," replied Del-mar in between licks.

***

All the Necessities

At least that beats the new business proposal Bubba's cousin, Junior, had come up with recently. Bubba said Junior was sticking up signs around town that read, *Valentine's Special! $500*.

When Bubba asked Junior what the special was, Junior told him, "I show up at your house in a full police uniform with blue lights flashing, arrest you in front of your wife and release you on Sunday."

"Who in the world is gonna want to do that?" asked Bubba skeptically.

Junior smiled, "You're missing the details here. The $500 includes a fishing license, poles, boat fees, tent, beers and all the necessities for the whole weekend."

"Oh, well, that makes sense then," said Bubba.

***

Circus Folk

Bubba told me a friend of his who works for the circus, wanted to adopt a child. He and his wife went to a local adoption agency and met with the Social workers there. The Social workers raised doubts about the living conditions in a circus, but the couple produced photos of their 50-foot luxury motor home, which was clean and well-maintained and equipped with a beautiful nursery.

The Social workers also raised concerns about the education a child would receive while in the couple's care.

"We've arranged for a full-time tutor who will teach the child all the usual subjects along with French, Mandarin Chinese and computer skills."

Next, the social workers expressed concern about a child being raised in a circus environment.

Bubba's friend and his wife told them, "Our nanny is a certified expert in Pediatric Care, Welfare and Diet."

The social workers were finally satisfied and asked, "What age child are you hoping to adopt?"

They said, "It doesn't really matter as long as they can fit in the cannon..."

***

Working at the Truck Stop

Bubba's best gal, Marg, said her cousin AnnaMae got a new job over at the DriveRite truck stop. You know, these truckers have their own language. *Chicken coop* means a weigh station, *smokey bear* refers to the police, etc.

Well, AnnaMae showed up her first day at the truck stop and one of the frequent drivers ordered 'four tires, three headlights turned on and four strips of rubber.' She had no idea what the trucker wanted but went to the back and repeated it to the greasy spoon cook.

The cook started laughing and said, "That means he wants four hot cakes, three eggs sunny side up and four pieces of bacon."

AnnaMae nodded and proceeded to grab a can of chili beans from the pantry. She took them back out front to the truck driver and set them on the table in front of him.

"What are these for?" asked the driver.

AnnaMae replied, "I just thought you might want to gas up while you're waiting on your other truck parts!"

***

Good Points / Bad Points

Troy Allen, Tiny's nephew, decided to try his hand at real estate. He completed his sales training but wasn't having much success selling. So going against his coaching, Troy Allen decided to be honest with a prospective house-buyer.

"This property has its good and bad points," stated Troy Allen.

The prospective buyer asked, "What are its bad points?"

"There is a chemical plant a half mile to the North and a chicken slaughterhouse a half mile to the South," said Troy Allen.

"Well, what are its good points?" asked the client.

Troy Allen replied, "You can always tell which way the wind is blowing."

And speaking of Troy Allen, he complained to his mom, Mavis Jean, that he could not get his new shoes on his feet lately. Mavis Jean asked him, "Did you break them in first?"

Troy Allen answered, "Well, not exactly but I've been putting on a clean pair of socks every day..." (Think about it...)

***

A Burglar?

Francine was telling her patrol partner, Eula, about a burglary scare they had the night before.

"I heard a noise, got up and saw a man's legs sticking out from under the bed," Francine shared.

Eula asked, "Was it the burglar?"

"No, it was my husband, Charles Thomas," replied Francine. "He'd heard the noise too."

***

The Office Job

Tiny said his nephew, Troy Allen, had recently landed his first office job. And, he was glad of it. Troy Allen said he'd had enough of working outside in all kinds of inclement weather. Now he was inside where it was warm and dry.

Well, the problem was since he hadn't worked in an office environment before, Troy Allen wasn't very familiar with office equipment. Copiers, fax machines and computers, etc., were all a bit new to him.

The second day on the job he found himself standing in front of the paper shredder looking a bit confused.

Luckily for him, one of the secretary's came along and asked him, "Do you need some help?"

"Yes," Troy Allen replied. "How does this thing work?"

"Simple," replied the secretary. She took the fat report from his hand and fed it into the shredder.

Appreciative as ever, Troy Allen said, "Thanks, but where do the copies come out?"

***

The Cleaning Lady

Bubba told me about the time they had tried out a cleaning lady at the farm. They hired this young gal to come by once a week and straighten things up a bit. They had agreed to pay her $50 a week; not overly generous but not peanuts either.

After a month, they decided it was just costing them too much and they informed the lady that they were going to have to let her go. They didn't think anything else about it until Bubba surmised the cleaning lady had taken a couple of their towels as a parting gesture.

"How dare she," Tiny protested. "Those were our two best towels!"

Bubba replied, "I know. One of them came from the Hilton hotel where we stayed last summer."

***

The New Client

You may remember dear reader that Bubba's cousin, Del-mar, recently started his own law firm by mailing out anonymous Valentine's Day cards. Well, a man came to see him at his Law office in the strip mall and told him, "My neighbor owes me $500 and he won't pay up. What should I do?"

"Do you have any proof he owes you the money?" asked Del-mar.

"Nope," replied the man.

Del-mar said, "OK, then write him a certified letter asking him for the $5,000 he owes you."

"But it's only $500," replied the man.

"Exactly. That's what he will reply and then you'll have your proof!"

***

In The Business

Tiny's friend, D-Wayne, who's in the furniture business, just got back from a trip to Paris, France. He stopped by the farm the other day to tell Tiny all about his visit.

D-Wayne said, "I met this little French girl while I was over there and we went out for dinner."

"That sounds nice," said Tiny. "What'd y'all talk about?"

"Well, I can't speak no French and she couldn't speak no English," answered D-Wayne.

Tiny took off his ball cap and scratched his head. "So, what'd you do?"

"After dinner, she got a pencil and drew a picture of a bed on the tablecloth," D-Wayne replied.

D-Wayne smiled as he recalled the memory, "You know, to this day, I can't figure out how she knew I was in the furniture business."

***

<u>Collection Notices</u>

Tiny and Bubba said their egg sales were doing well this past year. They have been selling to a number of the small grocers in the area. Tiny said most of them are prompt to pay their bills but a couple of them were significantly late.

They were trying to figure out how best to collect from these past-due accounts and developed the following statement that seemed to prove effective:

"If you refer to the date of our original invoice you will note that we have done more for you than your own mother. We have carried you for fourteen months!"

***

Unhappy Partnership

And speaking of uncles, Tiny's Uncle Merle was telling him about the time he was a partner in a trucking business. Merle's been driving big rigs all his life but about twenty years ago went into business with a partner named, Mr. Buckley. Merle supplied the labor and old Mr. Buckley supplied the truck.

By all accounts the partnership was an unhappy one from the get go. According to Merle, Mr. Buckley was tight as the bark on a tree and nickel and dimed him to death about his expenses out on the road.

One morning Merle called the front office from out on the road to check in and they reported Mr. Buckley had been taken to the hospital over night and was gravely ill. By the time Merle got back home from his latest run, Mr Buckley had taken a decided turn for the worse. Merle called the hospital to check on his condition. The head nurse on duty informed him, "I regret to tell you Mr. Buckley passed away just a few minutes ago."

The news stunned Merle for a moment as he put the telephone down. But, the next morning he again called the hospital and asked about Mr Buckley. The head nurse informed him, "Sir, Mr. Buckley passed away yesterday. We're sorry."

Well, beat it all if Merle didn't phone the hospital for a third time the next day and ask about Mr. Buckley's condition. The head nurse expressed some annoyance at Merle's call. "Sir, I've already told you twice that Mr. Buckley passed away. Why do you keep calling this hospital and asking about his condition?"

Merle replied with a sly grin, "I just like to hear it."

***

Ambition Can Take Flight

When Bubba's cousin, Del-mar graduated from Georgia Tech (the first one in the family to attend college), he told the family he was permanently moving to the big city of Orlando. The family didn't want him to go but Del-mar said he was an ambitious and talented person and the big city just has more opportunities for an educated person like himself.

So, Del-mar left home and moved to Orlando. Before long he had found a good job. He had been there about a month when he texted his mom:

Things are much better here like I told you. Already made supervisor. Feather in my cap!

A few weeks later he texted his mom again:

Already made manager. I told you things were better in the big city. Feather in my cap!

A few weeks later his mom got another text:

Fired from my job. Send money for ticket so I can come home.

Del-mar's mom texted back:

No ticket necessary - use your feathers to fly.

***

Business Plan

One of the farmers down the road from Tiny and Bubba decided they would go into town and try to get a loan to build a bathroom inside his house. Living out in the country all his life, the farmer had never been to a bank before. So, needless to say he was pretty nervous about the whole idea.

The farmer came straight to the point, "I want to borrow $1500 to put a bathroom in my house."

"I don't believe I know you," the bank president responded cautiously. "Do you mind telling where you've done your business before?"

The farmer replied, "Oh, out back in the woods."

***

The Fair Comes to Town

And speaking of older folks, the fair set up out past Lanier Village on the edge of Gainesville. You know how these carnivals travel around and set up for a few days and then move on.

Well, this carnival featured a 100 foot diving tower. A crowd gathered around waiting for the performer to come out. Finally, a feeble old man leaning on a cane approached the stage.

"Friends, I am ninety-nine years old and I am going to amaze you! I'm going to climb to the top of that tower and dive into this teeny-tiny tub of water."

The audience members begged him, "Don't do it, don't do it!"

"Okay," said the old man compliantly. "Next show at ten o'clock."

***

On Time

Tiny said he had several appointments in town lately and always tried to be on time. But, not everyone subscribes to this policy.

Frustrated, he said, "The trouble with being on time is that nobody's there to appreciate it."

***

Chapter 2 - Indonesia? Isn't that a Sleep Disorder?

Red and Bruised

That reminds me of the time Tiny said he went over to his sister, Mavis Jean's house. Troy Allen would have been a young boy, maybe ten or eleven years old. Tiny noticed Troy Allen's face was covered with red marks and bruises.

"What happened to Troy Allen, Mavis? His face is all red and bruised up. Did he get into a fight at school or something?" asked Tiny.

Mavis Jean shrugged, "No, we been trying to teach him to eat with a fork again."

***

Blondes in Cars... Speeding

Tiny's cousin, Francine, of Texas Highway Patrol fame, was out riding Interstate 35 last weekend with her partner, Eula, when they saw a car carrying two blondes blow past them at over 100 miles per hour.

The two troopers immediately gave chase and eventually got the blonde driver to slow down and stop.

Francine and Eula approached the car and asked for the driver's license and registration. Francine demanded, "Do you know how fast you were going?"

The blonde driver replied, "Well over a 100."

Eula asked, "Did you not see us following your car?"

"Well, to tell the truth," stated the blonde at the wheel, "I asked my friend here if she saw any cops following us?"

The blonde on the passenger's side spoke up, "I told her, 'As a matter of fact, I do.'"

Francine turned to the driver, "What did you say in response, m'am?"

"Oh, NOOOO!" yelled the blonde. "Are his flashers on?"

"And what did you say?" Eula questioned the blonde passenger.

"Yup...nope...yup...nope...yup..."

***

The One Right After 53

Marg and AnnaMae recently visited Washington, DC. This was their first time going to the city, and they really wanted to see the capitol building. They were checking their guide books but unfortunately, the pair couldn't find it (They are blonde after all). Finally Marg asked a police officer for directions.

"Excuse me, officer," the Marg said, "how do we get to the capitol building?"

The officer told them, "Wait here at this bus stop for the number 54 bus. It'll take you right there."

The blondes thanked the officer as he drove off.

Three hours later the police officer came back to the same area, and sure enough Marg and AnnaMae were still waiting at the same bus stop.

The officer got out of his car and asked, "Excuse me, but to get to the capitol building, I said to wait here for the number 54 bus. That was three hours ago. Why are you still waiting?"

AnnaMae piped up, "Don't worry, officer, it won't be long now. The 45th bus just went by!"

***

Comedy Clubs in North Georgia

And speaking of blondes, Marg and AnnaMae went to see a young ventriloquist who was touring the clubs, doing his show in some of the small towns in northeast Georgia. They were excited to be 'out on the town' and waited with anticipation as the show began. The pair had gotten to the club early and secured seats in the 2nd row.

With his dummy on his knee, the ventriloquist went through his usual dumb blonde jokes. Each joke seemed to build on the previous one, each making fun of blondes.

Finally, AnnaMae had had enough. She stood up on her chair and shouted, "I've heard enough of your stupid blond jokes! What makes you think you can stereotype women that way? What does the color of a person's hair have to do with her worth as a human being? It's guys like you who keep women like me from being respected at work and in the community, and from reaching our full potential as a person because you and your kind continue to perpetuate discrimination against, not only blondes but women in general... and all in the name of humor."

The embarrassed ventriloquist was quite taken aback and began to apologize. But AnnaMae was wound up by now and yelled again, "You stay out of this, mister! I'm talking to that little dummy on your knee!"

***

Crazy is As Crazy Does

Bubba said over at Amazon the other day a blonde office worker named Bonnie came out to the warehouse floor to walk around. The place is so big, lots of people there try to 'get their steps in' each day. As she was walking she looked up and saw Bubba's cousin, Del-mar, hanging upside down from an I-Beam in the ceiling.

Bonnie asked Del-mar, "What ARE you doing?"

Del-mar told her, "I need a few days off but the boss won't let me have them so I'm hanging upside down from this I-Beam acting crazy. The boss will see me, think I need rest and send me home for a few days."

Bonnie replied, "That won't work...uh ohh... here comes the boss now, you're in for it."

The boss spotted the blonde looking up and saw Del-mar hanging from the I-Beam and asked him, "Just WHAT do you think you are DOING?!!"

Del-mar said (in a "crazy" voice), "I'm a light bulb... I'm a light bulb."

The boss said, "Buddy, you need some rest... take the rest of today and tomorrow off and get some sleep."

As Del-mar was climbing down he winked at the blonde showing her it worked.

Bonnie thought about this for a moment and started to follow Del-mar out the door.

The boss asked her, "WHERE do you think YOU'RE going?"

Bonnie said, "I can't work in the dark."

***

Blonde Cash

Bubba's best girl, Marg, told him about one of her blonde girlfriend's who was down on her luck and needed money desperately.

To raise some quick cash, Reba decided to kidnap a child and hold him for ransom. She went to the local playground, grabbed a kid randomly, took him behind a building, and told the small boy, "I've kidnapped you."

Reba then wrote a big note saying, "I've kidnapped your kid. Tomorrow morning, put

$10,000 in a paper bag and leave it under the apple tree next to the slides, on the South side of the playground." Reba signed the note, "A blonde."

She then pinned the note to the kid's shirt and sent him home to show it to his parents.

The next morning, Reba checked, and sure enough, a paper bag was sitting beneath the apple tree. The blonde looked in the bag and found the $10,000 with a note that said, "How could you do this to a fellow blonde?"

***

Shed on Fire

Bubba said his blonde girlfriend, Marg, lives in a small house on the corner of 4th Avenue.

Marg had a small shed in her backyard where she kept her gardening tools. The other day, Marg thought she saw smoke coming out of the roof of her shed.

In a panic she called 911. A man answered and said, "This is Joe. Do you have an emergency?"

Marg hollered, "YES, MY SHED IS ON FIRE!!!"

Joe replied, "Don't panic. Help is on the way... Where do you live?"

Marg screamed, "IN A HOUSE. PLEASE HURRY!!"

Joe calmly responded, "How are we supposed to get there?"

The blonde Marg yelled, "DUH!!! IN A BIG RED TRUCK!"

***

House Fire

Tiny said recently his blonde cousin Thella's house had burned down. When she first spotted the fire, Thella had hung her head out the window and hollered to the neighbor, "My house is on fire!"

The neighbor hollered back, "Dial 9-1-1 and the Fire Department will come!"

Thella ducked back in the house grabbed the phone and tried and tried to dial the number. But, the Fire Department arrived too late and the house burnt down.

The neighbor asked Thella what had happened. Had she not called 9-1-1?

"I found the nine but I could never find the eleven," answered Thella.

***

Baby Doctor

Marg's blonde cousin, AnnaMae, accompanied her blonde friend, Maybelle, to the children's doctor recently. Maybelle had identical twin boys and it was their first trip to the pediatrician.

The waiting room was crowded and they ended up sitting on opposite sides of the room from each other, each holding one of the twins. A few minutes later another lady entered the waiting room. She sat down with her baby.

"It's amazing how much your babies look alike," commented the new mother, speaking to Maybelle and AnnaMae.

AnnaMae spoke right up, "They should. They both have the same father!"

Needless to say, the waiting room grew a little quieter as they sat there…

***

Call It Quits

And speaking of babies, Mavis Jean recounted how when she was pregnant with Suzie, her young son Troy Allen had overheard her and her husband (he who shall not be named…) talking about the upcoming birth.

Mavis Jean said a little chuckle welled up in her when she overheard Troy Allen telling one of his little friends about the new baby. The little friend asked Troy Allen, who was four at the time, if he was excited about the possibility of having a new brother or sister in the family.

"I sure am," Troy Allen was quick to answer. "And I already know what we're going to name it. If it's a girl, we're gonna call her Suzie. If it's a boy, we're gonna call it Quits..."

***

Out-of-Town Guest

Bubba's cousin, Junior, doesn't get out much. In fact just last month he stayed in an out-of-town hotel for the first time. It was quite an ordeal according to Junior. He showed up all tired from driving all day, checked in and went straight to his room. His dogs were whooped!

A few minutes later Junior called the front desk and shouted excitedly into the phone, "Help! I'm trapped inside my room!"

Not sure what to make of all the excitement, the hotel clerk asked Junior, "What do you mean *trapped*?"

"Well, I see three doors," Junior began. "The first door opens to a closet. The second door is to the bathroom. The third door has a *Do Not Disturb* sign hangin' on it."

***

White Lines

Tiny let his nephew, Troy Allen, borrow the pickup truck last week and he brought it back all banged up. Turns out he had been driving on the wrong side of the road.

Tiny asked him, "Troy Allen, didn't you see that white line down the middle of the highway? That's your guide. You stay on the right side and the people goin' the opposite direction stay on the other side of it."

Surprised, Troy Allen said, "I always thought that white line was for bicycles."

***

Minor Infraction

Bubba said his Uncle Fred told him about the time he went up north on vacation. He was somewhere in Pennsylvania when he noticed a blue light in his rear view mirror. He coasted over to the side of the road and waited for the highway patrolman to approach.

As the man came alongside Uncle Fred, Fred rolled down his car window. "You know you're driving without a taillight, sir."

Fred immediately got a little distraught. The Patrolman sensing Fred's anxiety said calmly, "Listen, it's not that big of a deal. It's a minor infraction."

Fred stepped out of the car and looked at the officer. "It may only be a minor infraction to you but to me it means I've lost my trailer, my wife, and my two kids."

***

What's Your Name?

Tiny said he visited his nephew, Troy Allen, over at Lanier Village last week. Now many of my dear readers know that Lanier Village is a fancy old folks home. And, they know that Troy Allen ain't even thirty yet. So, what he's doing over there?

He had gotten himself a job working in the kitchen. The pay weren't too bad and they got to eat a lot of leftovers. Anyway, Tiny sat there in the dining room and happened to overhear two elderly ladies visiting over their coffee.

"I've known you most of my life I reckon," said the first. "But, for the life of me, I can't remember your name. Would you please tell me what it is?"

The second lady sat there quietly for a moment and then asked, "How soon do you need to know?"

***

Fridge at the Shoe Store

Bubba Sr. said he went into a shoe store today that sells only shoes, nothing else. A young girl with a tattoo and green hair walked over to him and asked, "What brings you in today?"

He looked at her and said, "I'm interested in buying a refrigerator."

Bubba Sr. said she didn't quite know how to respond and had that 'deer in the headlights look...'

***

The New Horse

Bubba's best blonde girl, Marg, got a new horse. She rode it over to the farm. When she arrived, Bubba noticed she was sitting on the horse backwards.

"Why are you riding your horse backwards?" Bubba inquired.

Marg said, "It makes him nervous to have anyone looking over his shoulder."

***

Taking A Nap

Mavis Jean came into the living room and saw Suzie sitting there all quiet while her dad lay napping on the couch. A hint of pride overcame her as she said, "It's nice to see you sitting there so quiet while daddy's napping."

Suzie replied, "Yep, I'm watching his cigarette burn down to his fingers."

***

Chapter 3 - Are Cats Lazy? And Other Important Questions

The Barking Dog

Bubba's cajun brother-in-law, Boudreaux, and his sister Marie were lying in bed listening to the next door neighbor's dog. It had been in the backyard barking for hours and hours.

Finally, Marie jumped up out of bed and said, "I've had enough of this," and she went downstairs.

A few minutes later she finally came back up to bed and Boudreaux asked, "That dog is still barking. What have you been doing?"

Marie quipped smartly, "I put the dog in our backyard, let's see how THEY like it!"

***

Dead Dog

Tiny was telling about his Uncle Merle the other week. It seems Merle just can't seem to stay out of biker bars (or any bars for that matter). I guess it's part of the truck driver culture.

Anyway, Merle ventured into a biker bar in the Bronx and clearing his throat asked, "Um, err, which of you gentlemen owns the Doberman tied outside to the parking meter?"

A giant of a man, wearing biker leathers, his body hair growing out through the seams, turned slowly on his stool, looked down at Merle and said, "It's my dog. Why?"

"Well," blurted out Merle, "I believe my dog just killed it."

"What? No way!" roared the big man in disbelief. "What kind of dog do you have?"

Merle answered, "It's a little four week old female puppy."

"Bull!" growled the biker, "How could your puppy kill my Doberman?"

"Your dog choked on her."

***

And speaking of dogs, Bubba said he was sitting on the porch of the feed store a few days ago, waiting on Tiny to bring the pickup truck so they could load some chicken feed.

As he sat there another old farmer who obviously was making his annual trip to town was leaning on a post with his leashed dog which was just howling to beat the band. Bubba asked the mountain farmer why the dog was howling.

"Hookworm," said the farmer. "And, he's lazy."

"But," said Bubba, "I wasn't aware that the hookworm was painful."

"'Taint," responded the old farmer.

"Why, then," Bubba queried, "should the dog be howling?"

"Lazy."

"But why does laziness make him howl?" Bubba asked.

"Wal," said the old farmer, "that blame fool dawg is sittin' on a sand-bur, an' he's too tarnation lazy to get off, so he jes' sets thar an' howls 'cause it hurts."

***

Tame or Wild?

Tiny said they had hired a young boy from the city recently to help them out on the farm. They told the young man to be up and out at the chicken coop at 4 AM.

The next morning Tiny promptly went out to the coop and there was the young boy standing next to the entry door. He was yawning and rubbing his eyes as he tried focus in the darkness.

"Are these chickens tame or wild?" asked the boy.

Tiny smiled, "They're tame of course."

"Why are we sneaking up on them then?"

***

Lyin' Dog

When Bubba's cousin, Del-mar, went off to Georgia Tech, about a third of the way through the semester, he had foolishly squandered the money his parents had given him. Desperate to get more money from his dad, Lon, he came up with a sneaky plan. (Lon is the brother of Bubba's dad, Lum.)

Phoning home one weekend, Del-mar said, "Dad, you won't believe the educational opportunities that are available here at Georgia Tech! Why, they've even got a course here that will teach our dog, Pork Chop, how to talk!"

"That's amazin'!" said the gullible Lon. "How do I enroll him in the course?"

"Just send him down here with $1,000, and I'll make sure he gets in the course," said Del-mar.

So, Lon sent the dog and $1,000, but about two-thirds of the way through the semester, that money had also run out. Del-mar called his dad again.

"How's Pork Chop doing?" asked Lon.

"Awesome, Dad, Pork Chop's talking up a storm. You just won't believe this but they've had such great results with the talking dogs course that they're starting up a new one to teach dogs how to read!"

"Read?" echoed Lon. "You're kidding? What do I have to do to get him in that course?"

Del-mar replied, "Just send $2,500. I'll make sure Pork Chop gets in the course."

Lon duly sent the money, but at the end of the semester, Del-mar was faced with a problem: how to conceal from his dad the fact that Pork Chop could neither talk nor read. So, Del-mar decided to take drastic action and shoot the dog. When he came home for Christmas break, his dad was waiting expectantly.

"Where's Pork Chop?" asked Lon. "I can't wait to hear him talk or listen to him reading somethin'."

"Dad," said Del-mar solemnly, "I've got some bad news. This morning, when I got out of the shower, Pork Chop was in the living room reading the morning paper, like he usually does. Then suddenly he turned to me and asked, "So, is your Dad still messing around with that little blonde over at number 44?""

Lon's face turned red with rage and he shouted: "I hope you shot that lyin' dog!"

"I sure did, Dad," answered Del-mar.

"That's my boy!"

***

Animal Crackers

Tiny said when his nephew Troy Allen (That's Mavis Jean's boy), was young, he and his mom went to the grocery store. Not unusual in itself but upon their return home, Troy Allen found the bag with the box of animal crackers in it and immediately began emptying them out on the kitchen table.

Mavis Jean was a little surprised and asked him why.

Troy Allen had a concerned look on his face as he answered, "I'm looking for a seal."

"A seal?" asked Mavis Jean, pretty sure that was not one of the regular animals in the box of crackers.

Troy Allen replied, "The box says you should not eat it if the seal is broken, so I'm looking for the seal."

***

Grape Eating Duck

Bubba said his brother-in-law, Boudreaux, bought his son, Hebert, a pet duck. The cajun that sold Boudreaux this duck informed him the little paddle foot was unusual in that it only ate grapes. Hebert sure loved that animal and would take his duck everywhere on a leash.

One morning Hebert walked his duck into a store and asked the manager if they sold grapes. The manager said, "No, we don't sell grapes."

Hebert took the duck home but came back the next day and asked the same question. The manager answered the same thing again, "No, we do not sell grapes."

Hebert and the duck went home but were back again the next day, asking the manager if they sold grapes. The manager, exasperated, finally snapped and shouted, "No, we don't sell grapes! If you ask me one more time, I will nail your duck's beak to the floor!"

Hebert and the duck walked home. But they were back the next day. This time Hebert asked the store manager if he had any nails. The manager said, "No, I don't have any nails."

Hebert, standing there with the duck on a leash, replied, "Okay, good. Do you sell grapes?"

***

Chess-her Cat

Tiny said he met Merle the other night over at the Mall and Merle told him he had bought Aunt Tizzie a new cat. Seems Slug, her old cat, had finally moused out and went to that great cat heaven in the sky.

"This cat can play chess," Merle exclaimed proudly.

Tiny replied, "Really? That must be one smart cat."

"I ain't so sure about that," Merle clamored. "I usually end up winnin' three out of four games."

***

Going Somewhere

Tiny's friend, Junebug, runs the local pet store in Gainesville called Hairballs. Tiny said he was in the store the other day and noticed Junebug had pasted postcards around the outside of the goldfish bowls. The cards were all turned toward the inside of the tank.

"What's up with the postcards, Junebug? I see pictures of New York City, Florida and other vacation destinations."

Junebug smiled, "I watched them goldfish swimming round and round that tank everyday. I wanted them to think they was going somewhere."

***

Trick Dogs

Bubba's cousin, Junior's brother, Earl, is always a sucker for animal tricks. You may remember he bought a dancing duck one time. Recently he had gone to town and visited the jockey lot. A man there had three trick dogs. The man said, "Watch this," as he snapped his fingers.

The first dog did a flip and landed on his feet.

Earl said, "That ain't so hard. I've seen that done before."

The dog owner snapped his fingers again and the second dog did a flip and landed on top of the first dog's back.

Unimpressed, Earl said, "That ain't that hard either. I've seen it done before."

The man snapped his fingers a third time and the last dog turned a flip, landed on top of the back of the second dog and started singing the Star Spangled Banner. Now, he had Earl's attention.

"That was amazing. I want to buy that top dog!" Earl raved.

Smiling, the dog owner said, "No, you don't. You want the middle dog. He's a ventriloquist and he's throwin' his voice!"

***

The Duck Hunt

Tiny told me he and Bubba had gone duck hunting recently. Well, the first day out on the lake they didn't see a duck one.

They got up bright and early the next morning and went down close to the shore line. Tiny said they got their shotguns and were crawling on their bellies. A patch of grass here and a patch of grass there; Inching ever closer to some ducks they saw treading water. As they stood up to shoot, the ducks took flight before they could get a shot off.

Bubba decided they should go down to the local slaughterhouse and get themselves a cow hide. He reasoned they could wear the cow hide and the ducks would think it was a cow grazing.

They purchased a hide for $20 and the next morning Bubba got in the front and Tiny got in the back of the hide. They edged down to the water, pretending to pick grass and clover. A little grazing here, a little grazing there, inching ever closer to the flock of ducks they saw treading the water.

As they got close Bubba pulled out his shotgun. Tiny smacked him on the back and asked, "What are you doing? We need to get closer to the ducks!"

Bubba said, "Forget about the ducks. The bull is running this way."

***

Suzie's First Cat

Tiny recalled when his niece, Suzie, was four, she had a cat named Fluffy. She sure loved that cat but one day it got run over by a car.

Suzie's mom, Tiny's sister Mavis Jean, decided to quickly dispose of the remains before Suzie found out about it.

After a few days, Suzie finally asked about the cat.

"Suzie, the cat died," Mavis Jean explained. "But it's all right. He's up in heaven with God."

Suzie asked, "What in the world would God want with a dead cat?"

***

Free Ride

Bubba said he was out fishing all morning over at Lanier the other day and didn't get a single bite. Talk about being discouraged, tired and frustrated. After several hours, he decided just to pack it in. There's always tomorrow.

He started his motor and headed slowly for shore. All of the sudden he heard a big thump in the boat! He turned around and there was a huge bass laying in the bottom of his boat!

Bubba stopped, reached back, grabbed the fish and threw it back in the lake! "You didn't wanna get in my boat all day so don't think you're gonna get a free ride now!"

***

Mouser

Bubba's sister, Marie, told him she answered the doorbell the other morning at their bayou home and a city slicker man was standing on her front porch.

The man said, "I'm terribly sorry. I just ran over your cat and I would like to replace it for you."

Marie replied, "Well, that's alright by me. How are you at catching mice?"

***

Chapter 4 - Don't Make Me Use My Preacher Voice

Is This Heaven?

Boudreaux lay dying in his bed. Bubba said they know'd he was dying because he had told his sweet wife Marie, "I'm dying."

As he lay there, death's agony was suddenly pushed aside as he smelled the aroma of his favorite homemade chocolate chip cookies wafting up the stairs.

Gathering his remaining strength, he lifted himself from the bed. Leaning against the wall, he slowly made his way out of the bedroom, and with intense concentration, supported himself down the stairs, gripping the railing with both hands. In labored breath, he leaned against the door frame, gazing wide-eyed into the kitchen.

There, spread out upon newspapers on the kitchen table were literally HUNDREDS of his favorite chocolate chip cookies!

Was it heaven? Or, was it one final act of heroic love from his devoted wife, seeing to it that he left this world a happy man?

Mustering one great final effort, Boudreaux threw himself toward the table, landing on his knees in a rumpled posture, one hand on the edge of the table. The unsteady hand quiveringly made its way to a cookie near the edge of the table; feeling the warm soft dough actually made the pain of his bones subside for a moment. His parched lips parted; the wondrous taste of the cookie was already in his mouth; seemingly bringing him back to life.

What, then, was this sudden stinging that caused his hand to recoil?

Boudreaux looked to see his wife, Marie, still holding the spatula she had just used to smack his hand.

"Stay out of those!" Marie said, "They're for the funeral."

***

Desperate to Win

Bubba said his best girl, Marg, told him she was really concerned about her blonde girlfriend, AnnaMae. It seems AnnaMae had lost her job at the dress shop and had gotten herself into a little financial trouble.

AnnaMae told Marg things had gotten so bad she had started asking the Lord to help her win the Lottery. But, the other night they drew the numbers and somebody else won.

AnnaMae said she doubled down on her prayers, telling the Lord, 'If I don't win the Lottery I'm gonna lose my house and my car. Please Lord, let me win the Lottery.'

But, again another drawing had come and gone and AnnaMae didn't win. She told Marg she was plumb distraught over the whole thing.

AnnaMae started asking the Lord 'why He had forsaken her when she had always been a good Christian, went to church regularly and gave her old clothes to Goodwill. Please Lord let me win the Lottery so I can get my life back on track.'

It was then AnnaMae said she had a flash of revelation. It was almost as if the heavens opened and she heard the Lord say to her, "AnnaMae, work with me on this... Buy a ticket."

***

Help! I've Fallen and I Can't Get Up

Bubba said his pastor from Third Baptist, Preacher Davis, had recently made friends with an old priest over at the local Catholic church. They often talked about the differences in worship in their respective churches. Bubba's preacher asked the priest about Confession and how that all worked. The old priest explained the process of Confession but admitted he was getting sick and tired of all the people in his parish who kept confessing adultery. In fact, one Sunday in the pulpit he told his flock, "If I hear one more person confess to adultery, I'll quit!"

Everyone liked the old priest, so the parishioners came up with a code word. Someone who had committed adultery would say they had "fallen." This seemed to satisfy the old priest and things went well, until the priest died at a ripe old age.

About a week later, the new priest visited the Mayor of the town and seemed very concerned. The young priest said, "You have to do something about the sidewalks in town. When people come into the confessional, they keep talking about having fallen."

The Mayor started to laugh, realizing that no one had told the new priest about the code word.

The priest shook an accusing finger at the mayor and said, "I don't know what you're laughing about. Your wife fell three times this week."

***

Redneck Church

Bubba said he visited a redneck church a couple Sundays back. He had gone out of town for a Feed and Seed show and just popped in the back pew as the service was getting started. Tiny asked him how he reckoned it was a redneck church. Bubba said there were some telltale signs including:

- The preacher was preaching on Jesus feeding the 5,000 with the two fishes and 12 loaves. Someone asked if the fish were bass or catfish and what was the bait used.
- There was a special fund raiser for a new church septic tank.
- The high notes on the organ set the dogs on the floor to howling.
- One member of the church requested to be buried in his 4-wheel-drive truck because, 'It ain't never been in a hole it couldn't get out of.'
- The final words of the preacher's benediction were, "Y'all come back now, ya hear?"

Bubba did say he felt at home though when they took up the offering. The pastor asked, "Will Bubba help take up the offering?"

Five guys and two women stood up...

***

Red Wagon Hostage

Bubba said he and Tiny had a little family gathering a few days ago. Families seem to do this occasionally as Christmas approaches. Tiny's sister Mavis Jean was there and she shared about the time her little Suzie wanted a red wagon for Christmas.

"She was desperate for this red wagon we'd seen over at the Mall. I told her to write a letter to Santa about it," Mavis Jean started.

"Well, you know Suzie, she had to go one better..."

"Dear Jesus," she wrote. "If I get a red wagon for Christmas, I won't fight with my brother Troy Allen for a year." Then Suzie thought, '*Oh, no, Troy Allen is such a brat, I could never, ever keep that promise*.' So, Suzie threw away the letter and started again.

"Dear Jesus, if I get a red wagon for Christmas, I will eat all my vegetables for a year." Then Suzie thought, '*Oh, no, that means spinach, broccoli and 'paragus. Yuck! I could never ever keep that promise.*'

Suddenly, Suzie had a bright idea. She went downstairs to the living room. From the mantel above the wood stove, she grabbed the family's statue of the Virgin Mary from Mavis

Jean's Nativity scene. Taking the statue to the kitchen she wrapped it in newspapers and stuffed it into a Walmart bag. She took the bag upstairs to her room, opened the closet and placed the bag in the darkest back corner.

Once she got the door closed, she took out a new sheet of paper and wrote, "Dear Jesus, if you ever want to see your mother again..."

After listening to the story Tiny said, "Yep, that sounds like Suzie..."

***

<u>Women Pallbearers</u>

Tiny's grandma Cledy, said she had tried all the different dating apps and never got a single bite. Her husband has been dead for years and she was trying to get back into the dating scene without much luck.

Starting to feel a little past her sell-by date, Cledy visited the local funeral home and pre-paid her final expenses. Next, she went to Preacher Davis and told him how she wanted her funeral done.

"I want nothing but women pallbearers for my funeral, preacher," said Cledy.

The preacher asked Cledy, "Why on earth would you want that?"

"Them men wouldn't take me out when I was alive," Cledy protested. "I sure ain't gonna let them take me out after I'm dead!"

***

Hungry and Cold

Junior, Bubba's cousin on his mom's side, had an accident at the chicken processing plant and fell into a deep coma. It was feared that he would soon be deceased.

Just when it appeared all hope was lost, Junior made a remarkable recovery. Soon, he was receiving friends and relatives in his hospital room. Bubba asked him what it felt like to be practically dead.

"Dead? I never really worried about it because I was hungry and my feet were cold," replied Junior.

Bubba pressed Junior, "How would that make you so sure you weren't dead?"

"Well, I knew that if I was in Heaven, I wouldn't be hungry. And, if I was in the other place, my feet definitely wouldn't be cold."

Bubba said he couldn't argue with Junior's logic.

***

Mountain Livin'

Tiny recounted how his two West Virginia friends, Homer and Hector, had pretty much lived their entire lives in the mountains. (You may recall them doing a little panhandlin' from another book...). Anyway, Hector and Homer were walking to town one day when they met a Catholic priest whose arm was in a sling.

Hector asked the priest, "Priest, what happened to your arm?"

"I slipped and fell in the bathtub," came the reply from the priest as he continued on his way.

The boys had walked a little piece on down the road when Hector said to Homer, "What's a bathtub anyway?"

"How should I know," answered Homer. "I ain't no Catholic!"

***

Christmas Trivia

Bubba said he and Marg were at church last Sunday and Pastor Davis decided to play a little impromptu game of Christmas trivia during the service. The game went on for a couple of quick rounds and it came down to Marg and one other lady contestant.

"To be today's winner," Pastor Davis smiled, "name two of Santa's reindeer."

Marg, who was to be first to answer, gave a sigh of relief, gratified that she had drawn such an easy question. "Rudolph!" she said confidently, "and... Olive!"

The congregational audience started to applaud but the clapping quickly faded into mumbling. The confused Pastor replied, "Yes, we'll accept Rudolph, but could you please explain 'Olive'?"

"You know," Marg began to sing circling her hand forward impatiently,

"Rudolph the Red Nosed Reindeer had a very shiny nose. And if you ever saw it, you would even say it glows. Olive, the other reindeer..."

After church as they were headed to get something to eat, Marg told Bubba she really didn't need that vase of poinsettias anyway. Where in the world would she put them?

***

Creation VS Evolution?

Bubba said he remembers as a child asking his parents how people were born. He went to his mom first and said, "How were people born?" His mom, Daisy, said, "Adam and Eve made babies, then their babies became adults and made babies, and so on."

Bubba said he then went to his dad, Lum, and asked him the same question and he told him, "We were monkeys then we evolved to become like we are now."

Bubba said he ran back to his mom and said, "You lied to me!"

His mom replied calmly, "No, your dad was talking about his side of the family."

***

Dead Rat

Tiny recounted how one day Preacher Davis stopped by to visit his sister, Mavis Jean. They hadn't been talking long when her daughter, Suzie, showed up proudly holding a big dead rat by the tail.

Suzie stated with an air of confidence, "Oh, it's dead alright, Mama. We beat it and beat it and beat it. It's deader 'n dead."

Mavis Jean's eyes glanced over at the preacher, then back to Suzie. Suzie decided something a little more dignified and reverent was needed because of Pastor Davis's presence.

She solemnly intoned, "Yes, we beat it and beat it until the Lord called it home."

***

Where Is My Paper?

Bubba said his grandpa, Bubba Sr, got all tied up in knots the other week. It seems he called the Gainesville Times newspaper offices and loudly demanded to know where his Sunday edition was.

'Sir," said the newspaper employee, "Today is Saturday. The Sunday paper is not delivered 'til Sunday."

There was a quiet pause on the other end of the phone, followed by a bolt of recognition.

"So... that's why no one was in church today..."

***

New Commandment

The Sunday School teacher over at Third Baptist was discussing the Ten Commandments with her five and six year olds.

After explaining the commandment to "honor thy father and thy mother," she asked, "Is there a commandment that teaches us how to treat our brothers and sisters?"

Without missing a beat Suzie answered, "Thou shall not kill."

***

The Atheist

One of Marg's girlfriends got married recently. She returned from the honeymoon all distressed. As she shared the details with Marg and the mother-in-law, she exclaimed, "Living with Bill is going to be horrible. He says he's an atheist and doesn't believe in a place called Hell."

The girl broke down in tears. Her mom put her arms around her shoulder and told her, "Don't worry, baby. Between you and me, we'll have no trouble showing him how wrong he is."

***

Cowboys and Indians

Bubba said his Grandpa Bubba Sr went to visit his sister Marie who lives in Louisiana. Marie's three kids were all still young. Bubba Sr came in the kitchen one morning and Hebert, Marie's youngest, was crying.

"What's the matter, Hebert?" asked Bubba Sr.

Hebert sniffled, "Daddy won't play Cowboys and Indians with me."

"Don't cry. I'll play with you," replied Bubba Sr.

Hebert sighed, "That's no good, Grandpa. You've already been scalped."

***

Chapter 5 - Love is Like A Toothache...

Guns and Marriage

Tiny said he was talking with his uncle Merle the other day. They were talking men-talk - sports, guns and women. The subject of marriage came up as they spoke about firearms.

Merle told Tiny, "You'd be smart to marry a short woman."

"Why is that, Uncle Merle?" Tiny asked.

"Well, you could put your guns up high on a shelf where she couldn't reach them if she ever got mad at you," Merle answered.

Tiny scratched his head and pondered, "What difference would that make? She could always get a chair and grab one."

"True," said Merle. "But, at least you'd hear her dragging the chair."

***

A Strange Donation

Bubba was visiting his uncle Fred last week. Fred's getting up there in years and has always had a taste for a drink or two. Bubba said they had been sitting and talking for a while when he noticed his aunt, Fred's wife Evelyn, wasn't around.

Bubba asked Fred where his wife was and Fred replied, "She went with the people who rang the doorbell earlier."

"The people who rang the doorbell?" Bubba asked, wondering if Fred wasn't a little muddled by a sip or two of something stronger than water.

Fred replied matter-of-factly, "Yep, they came by and said they was collecting for the Old Folks home. So, I gave 'em Evelyn."

***

Stitch in Time

Bubba Sr was sitting in the living room of the retirement home with his friend, Jerome, when one of the female residents ran down the hallway without a stitch of clothing on. The two men just looked at each other.

"Who was that?" asked Jerome.

Bubba Sr replied, "I don't know but whatever she was wearing looked like it sure needed ironing."

***

Beautiful Flowers

And speaking of Valentine's Day, Francine, Tiny's cousin of Texas Highway Patrol fame, called her husband, Charles Thomas, on that special day and told him, "Three of the girls in my office just received some flowers for Valentine's Day. They are absolutely gorgeous!"

Charles Thomas as usual spoke without considering the consequences. "That's probably why they received them then."

Needless to say, he ended up eating a TV dinner that evening…

***

Tell the Truth

Tiny was telling me how his niece, Suzie, really embarrassed her mom, Mavis Jean, when her friend Maybelle came over to visit. Of course, Suzie is known to tell the truth, whatever the situation, (You may remember dear reader all the trouble she had with her grade school teacher regarding her favorite animal - chicken!).

Upon seeing the woman, Suzie turned to Maybelle and said: "My Goodness, you're ugly!"

Her mother overheard the remark and was appalled.

Mavis Jean took Suzie to one side and gave her a real telling-off before ordering her to go back and say she was sorry to Maybelle.

Suitably chastened, the girl went over and said quietly:

"Maybelle, I'm sorry you're ugly."

***

The Key to Understanding Women

Tiny said he was visiting his cousin, Francine, last week out in Texas. They had several of the family members over for Sunday dinner, including Francine's father-in-law, Hershel. (You may remember Hershel had a problem with his chainsaw a while back...).

Anyway, the men folk got to bragging as they are wont to do and Hershel recalled the advice he had given to his son, Charles Thomas, before his marriage to Francine. Hershel explained that communication was a priority in a marriage and there were several key words a husband needed to listen for because they had special meaning to women.

"For instance?" Charles Thomas asked.

"Well, take the word, 'Fine,' replied Hershel. "When a woman says, 'fine' it really means, 'I am right. This argument is over. You need to shut up.'"

Charles Thomas shook his head and queried, "What else?"

"There's the phrase, 'That's okay.' This is one of the most dangerous statements a woman can make to a man. "That's okay" means she wants to think hard and long before deciding when and how you'll pay for your mistake," Hershel told his son.

"Any other words I need to be aware of?" asked Charles Thomas.

Hershel replied, "Yep, one more. 'Nothing.' When she says 'nothing,' this is the calm before the storm. This means 'Something' and you better be on your toes. Note: Arguments that start with 'Nothing' usually end with 'Fine.'"

Francine was watching all this and offered up her own thoughts on the matter. "It ain't really a word but if you hear a woman give a 'loud sigh.' This is a non-verbal cue often misunderstood by men. It means I think you're are an idiot and wonder why I'm standing here wasting my time arguing with you about 'Nothing.'"

***

The Key to Understanding Men

Speaking of Francine, she offered her marital wisdom to a couple of her female colleagues at the Texas Highway Patrol the other morning. She and Charles Thomas have been married for several years now and she fancies herself an expert of sorts on marital bliss.

"There are six rules to always remember when asking a man to do something," Francine stated.

"First, Make sure the man is conscious."

"Second, if you have trouble getting his attention, crash the hard drive on his computer and line the bird cage with the sports section."

"Third, be brief! Limit your nagging speech to two, three hours, max."

"Fourth, try rewarding him for cooperative behavior. Offer to cook him something that doesn't have a peel-back cover."

"Fifth, if he refuses to cooperate, punish him by microwaving his TV remote on high for 30 minutes. Rotate 1/4 turn, and microwave again for another 30 minutes."

"Lastly, if all else fails, try using "would you" or "will you" instead of "you'd better" or "do as I say and no one will get hurt."

Francine's female colleagues nodded in agreement. Yes, she had marriage all figured out...

***

Right Temperature for A Bath

When Tiny's cousin Francine and her husband, Charles Thomas got their new little Japanese baby boy from the Adoption Agency, like most new parents, they had all kinds of questions.

One question was how to know if they had the right temperature for the baby's bath water. Francine thought she'd better check with an expert, so she called up their Aunt Cledy who'd already raised two sons, Cletus and Wade.

Cledy told Francine, "Put the baby in the bath water. If he turns red, it's too hot. If he turns blue, it's too cold. If the water turns black, he really needed a bath."

That's the benefit of asking an expert...

***

Stop Fussin'

Tiny said his grandma Cledy visited the other day. Not one for tact or discretion, she asked his sister, Mavis Jean, straight off if she and her husband still fussed a lot.

"Mavis, do you and your husband still quarrel now same as you used to?"

"No, we sure don't, ma'am," Mavis replied.

A smile crossed Cledy lips, "That's good. I bet you're glad of that, ain't you?"

"Yes, ma'am, I sure am!" answered Mavis.

Cledy asked, "What caused y'all to stop fussin', Mavis?"

"He died."

***

Pearls of Wisdom

Mavis Jean told Tiny the other week she had been to visit Aunt Tizzie. Tizzie was sitting there knitting as Mavis Jean and a couple of her female cousins listened to the old woman dispense relationship wisdom.

"Men," Tizzie proceeded to expound, "are guilty of three great follies."

The cousins listened intently as Tizzie laided out her case regarding the opposite sex. "The first is they will climb a tree to shake down the fruit, when if they would wait, the fruit would fall on its own."

"That's exactly right," agreed Mavis Jean as the other two cousins nodded. "They can't wait for nothin.'"

Tizzie continued, "Second, they go to war to kill one another, when if they would only wait, they would surely die naturally."

"You got that right," Mavis pattered. "They are always in a hurry to start something."

The cousins leaned in expecting another great pearl of wisdom to drop from the old lady's lips. "Lastly," Tizzie started, "they run after women, when, if they did not do so, the women would surely run after them."

Mavis Jean and her two cousins had to admit the old woman was right, especially her last point.

***

Business Trip Divorce

Bubba's cousin, Del-mar, recounted why he had filed for a divorce from his wife. 'Course his wife was from Lula and her dad was a big time businessman there who had offered Del-mar a job as a traveling salesman.

Normally, Del-mar finished his calls on Friday and came home. On one of his sales trips he had finished early and sent his wife a text that he would be coming home on Thursday.

He arrived home Thursday, parked his pickup truck and walked up to the house. He looked through the picture window and saw his wife in the arms of another man. Rather than go into the house, Del-mar went down the block to talk to the father-in-law.

"I ain't gonna stand for this. I'm filing for a divorce in the morning," hollered Del-mar.

The father-in-law tried to calm Del-mar down, "Let's not be too hasty. Let me go down there and talk to her and see if I can figure out what's going on. There must be a good reason."

So, the father-in-law visited the daughter and came back about twenty minutes later. "I knew there'd be a good reason. She didn't get your text..."

***

First Dance
Tiny's sister, Mavis Jean, said her young daughter, Suzie, went to her first dance the other night. A young boy was picking her up. Mavis Jean told Suzie all about social graces.

"He's probably gonna be very nervous so say something nice to put him at ease," Mavis told her.

The young lad showed up and Suzie got in his beater of a car. They arrived at the dance and went inside. Later, while they were dancing, Suzie remembered her mother's words of wisdom and finally commented:

"For a fat boy you sure don't sweat much!"

***

Need A Compliment?
Tiny said his cousin Francine was feeling all down and out the other day. She sat in front of the mirror and complained to her husband, Charles Thomas, "I'm getting all fat and ugly. I sure could use a compliment about now."

Charles Thomas, not always the sharpest tool in the shed, replied, "I'd say your eyesight is spot on."

Needless to say he had TV dinners the next several days...

***

Plastic Surgery

But, that ain't as bad as what Bubba's uncle Fred told his wife, Evelyn. She was complaining she wanted him to pay for some plastic surgery; in particular a face-lift.

Fred said he would do that. "In fact," Fred replied, "I'd love to have a new pair of boots."

Aunt Evelyn was a little slow off the draw. "Boots? What's boots have to do with me getting a face-lift?"

"I figure you're gonna have enough skin left over for me to get a pair of boots made," Fred laughed.

Straight to the doghouse. Do not pass GO... Do not collect $200 dollars.

***

Country Funeral

Tiny told me he and Bubba had attended a funeral last week. One of the old farmers in the community had passed away. The man was known to be a little bit of a ruffian but Preacher Davis volunteered to have his funeral at Third

Baptist anyway. The Preacher told Tiny, 'Everybody deserves a good send off regardless of their eventual destination...'

Well, the day of the funeral, the family had gathered - the man had a wife and five kids. Preacher Davis was upfront speaking kind words about the deceased.

"He was an honest man, a faithful husband and a good father," said Preacher Davis.

Tiny said he and Bubba were sitting right behind the widow. When she heard the preacher say this, the widow leaned over to one of her kids, "Run up there and check that casket and make sure it's your Pa in there."

***

Candy Bar Defense

I told you a while back that Del-mar, Bubba's cousin on his dad Lum's side, had went into lawyering. (He's the one who sent out all them Valentine's Day cards with 'Guess Who?' written on them). Anyway, he finally got a client. It was an old fella up in the mountains who was seeking a divorce from his young wife.

The trial was being held locally way up in the mountains and the couple was really arguing over custody of their kids. The mother jumped to her feet and protested to the judge, "Since I'm the one who brought these kids into the world, I should get to keep them!"

The judge cautioned her to sit down as he asked for the old mountain man's side of the story. The man wanted the children as well.

After a long moment of silence, Del-mar, who was representing the old mountain man, pushed his chair back and rose to his feet. "Your honor, when I put a quarter in a candy machine and a candy bar comes out, does it belong to me or the candy machine?"

I never did hear how the Judge ruled...

***

Autumn Romance

Marg, Bubba's best girl told her cousin, AnnaMae, that a while back, when it was a nice warm Autumn evening, she and Bubba were sitting in the swing out on the front porch. They had sat there a while, kind of romantic like and Marg noticed Bubba getting all red-faced and starting to mop sweat off his brow.

"I just knew he was gonna propose to me," Marg said as she recounted the story to AnnaMae.

"What did he say?" asked AnnaMae.

Marg answered, "He was kind of quiet, just squirmmin' and moppin' sweat. I figured I'd help him out so I told him, 'It's gettin' late.'"

AnnaMae smiled, "Then what did he say?"

"He pulled his handkerchief out, wiped his brow and said, 'It ain't that. It's just too early for this long underwear.'"

***

Golf Fanatic

One of Tiny's good friends is an absolute golf fanatic. All he talks about 24/7 is golf. Golf, golf, golf. He is eat up with it. The friend just got married.

Tiny said he confessed to his new bride on his wedding night, "Honey, I should have told you I'm an avid golfer. I hope you won't be too upset if you don't see me much on the weekends."

The young bride replied sweetly, "Well, as long as we're making confessions, you should know that I was a hooker."

Not missing a beat, the friend replied, "Oh, that's nothing to worry about."

He went on, "We can fix that by moving your right hand a little on the grip and dropping your left foot back..."

***

Annual Physical
Bubba's Aunt Evelyn accompanied her husband, Fred, to the doctor for his annual physical exam. After about thirty minutes, the doctor came out to speak with Evelyn.

"I don't like the way your husband looks," he began.

Evelyn piped up, "Neither do I but he's pretty handy around the house."

***

Perfect Man
Tiny's blonde cousin, Francine, who still works for the Texas Highway Patrol, had one of her work friends over the other evening for supper. The talk turned as it is wont to do to men-folk.

The young woman expounded, "The man that I marry has to be a shining light when we're around company. He must be musical. Sing. Stay home at night."

Francine's husband, Charles Thomas, overheard this cynical discussion and commented, "Lady, what you really want is a TV not a man..."

***

Changeable Man

Tiny said his Aunt Cledy was recently dishing out marital advice to her two daughter-in-laws (they had married her sons, Cletus and Wade). Anyway, the subject of men came up and the talk turned to the age-old question, 'Can you change a man?'

Cledy advised with a nod, 'The only way you can change a man is if he is in diapers."

***

And speaking of women dishing out marital advice, Bubba's gal, Marg, had lunch with her blonde cousin, AnnaMae, the other day at Cracker Barrel. AnnaMae told Marg she had met a man recently that she really wanted to impress.

"What do I do if he asks me what sort of books I'm interested in?" AnnaMae queried.

Marg replied as she lifted a forkful of okra to her mouth, "Tell him checkbooks."

***

Diagnosis?

That ain't nothing. When Tiny's Uncle Merle went to the doctor, the doc checked him out and told him he couldn't find anything wrong with him. He did tell him though, "I do recommend that you give up half your love life."

"Which half do you suggest, Doc," Merle replied. 'Thinkin' about it or talkin' about it?"

***

Chapter 6 - What if Algebra Teachers Are Really Pirates?

Math Homework

Bubba's sister, Marie, recalled the time their son, Hebert, was struggling with his math homework from school.

He was sitting at the kitchen table and after a while, he turned to his father, Boudreaux and said, "Dad, can you help me?"

Boudreaux said: "I could. But it wouldn't be right, would it?"

"Probably not," said Hebert. "But you could at least give it a try."

***

My Brother's Boots
Suzie's old elementary school teacher was helping one of her kindergarten students put his boots on. It had been getting colder outside and the kids were starting to dress for the weather.

He had asked for help and she could see why. With her pulling and him pushing, the boots still didn't want to go on. When the second boot was on, the teacher had worked up a sweat. She almost whimpered when the little boy said, "Teacher, they're on the wrong feet."

She looked, and sure enough, they were. It wasn't any easier pulling the boots off than it was putting them on. The teacher managed to keep her cool as together they worked to get the boots back on - this time on the right feet.

He then announced, "These aren't my boots."

The teacher bit her tongue rather than get right in his face and scream, "Why didn't you say so?" like she really wanted to do. Once again she struggled to help him pull the ill-fitting boots off.

The little boy then said, "They're my brother's boots. My Mom made me wear them."

The teacher didn't know if she should laugh or cry. She then mustered up the grace to wrestle the boots onto his feet again.

"Now, where are your mittens?" the teacher asked.

He said, "I stuffed them in the toes of my boots..."

***

Counting Cats

Tiny recounted how Suzie had another fuss with her Elementary school teacher. Yep, it's that same teacher that sent her to the principal after she said fried chicken was her favorite animal. Anyway, the teacher was trying to illustrate a math problem and stated, "If I gave you 2 cats and another 2 cats and 2 more, how many would you have?"

Suzie answered, "Seven."

"No, listen carefully... If I gave you two cats, and another two cats and another two, how many would you have?" asked the teacher.

Suzie answered, "Seven."

The teacher was slowly growing frustrated as she said, "Let me put it to you differently. If I gave you two apples, and another two apples and another two, how many would you have?"

"Six," answered Suzie.

"Okay, good. Now, if I gave you two cats, and another two cats and another two, how many would you have?"

Suzie answered, "Seven."

The teacher exploded, "Suzie, where in the world do you get seven from?!"

"Because I've already got a cat!"

***

Prone to Streeeeetch Things

Tiny said his nephew Troy Allen, Mavis Jean's boy, was prone to exaggeration and truth-stretching when he was younger. His Elementary school teacher noticed this tendency about him and decided to try and break it.

That morning when Troy Allen came into class the teacher told him, "Troy Allen, I looked out my back window this morning and saw the biggest black grizzly bear I've ever seen. It was going through my trash. About that time, a small brown dog came around the corner, grabbed that bear by the leg and drug him clean out of the trash can. They fought and do you know that little brown dog killed that big black bear right then and there. Can you believe that?"

"I sure do," Troy Allen spoke up. "That's my little brown dog and that's the third bear he's killed this week!"

The teacher decided it was time to give up...

***

Cards for Every Occasion

Bubba said Marg's little niece, Jessie Jewel, was recently with them out at the Mall. They took her out there to give her some space to roam around while they watched her from a short distance away. They were surprised to see her standing in front of a shop that had a sign in the window, "Cards for every occasion."

As they looked on, Jessie Jewel stepped inside the shop and started pouring over the stock of cards. After a while, one of the clerks came over to her and asked, "What kind of card are you looking for little girl? We've got cards for every occasion. A card for a little sick friend? An Anniversary card for your ma and pa?"

"No," Jessie Jewel shook her head. "Have you got anything in the line of blank report cards?"

***

Neat Freak

Tiny said he watched while his nephew, Troy Allen, Mavis Jean's boy, filled out a college questionnaire to help him determine a compatible roommate. Beside the questions, "Do you make your bed regularly?" and "Do you consider yourself a neat person?" Troy Allen had checked, YES.

Tiny had been watching over Troy Allen's shoulder and knowing him a little better asked him why he had lied.

"If I tell the truth, they're liable to put me with some slob."

***

First Kiss

When Tiny's seven-year-old niece, Suzie, got home from school, she told her mother, Mavis Jean, that Tommy had kissed her after class.

"How did that happen?" asked Mavis Jean, shocked.

"It wasn't easy," Suzie said. "Three other girls had to hold him down for me!"

***

Clothes Tag

Troy Allen, Tiny's nephew, has had his trouble with washing machines in the past. But, he stopped by his mom's house the other day after work and decided to wash his sweatshirt. He trudged down the stairs into the basement and pulled off the garment.

"What setting do I use on the washing machine ?" he hollered back up the stairs to his mom.

Mavis Jean replied, "What does it say on your sweatshirt?"

"University of Georgia."

***

Football for the Elderly

Bubba said his mom, Daisy, and her older sister Sadie, recently donated $5 to a charity and to their surprise, won tickets to a University of Georgia football game.

Since they had never seen a live football game before, Daisy thought the free tickets would be an excellent opportunity to do so.

"Me too," said Sadie. "Let's go!"

They soon found themselves high up in noisy Sanford Stadium overlooking a large, grassy expanse. The elderly women watched the kickoff and the seemingly endless back-and-forth struggles that comprised the scoreless first half. They enjoyed the UGA band music and cheerleader performance that followed.

Then came the second half. When the teams lined up for the second-half kickoff, Daisy nudged her sister. "I guess we can go home now, Sadie," she said. "This is where we came in."

***

Watch That Perfume

When Suzie, Tiny's niece, was seven, her mom, Mavis Jean bought her a watch and bottle of perfume for her birthday. Suzie was so excited about her gifts she pestered everyone in earshot about them.

"See my watch? Smell my perfume!" exclaimed Suzie. She was really getting on people's last nerve.

Mavis Jean told Suzie the preacher was coming over later that evening for dinner. "Don't be bothering him with all this talk about your watch and that perfume," Mavis said.

Suzie was careful to obey her mom. But, while they were sitting at the table, Suzie couldn't stand it anymore. She told the preacher, "I'm not supposed to talk about it. But, anything you hear or anything you smell, it's me!"

***

The Tooth Fairy

Tiny recalled how when his nephew, Troy Allen, was a youngster, he became more curious about the mysterious tooth fairy.

He lost another one of his baby teeth and finally putting two and two together, he came right out and asked his mom at the breakfast table, "Mom, are you the tooth fairy?"

Assuming he was old enough to hear the truth, Tiny's sister, Mavis Jean, replied, "Yes, Troy Allen, I am."

Troy Allen seemed to take this news pretty well. He quietly finished his cereal and grabbed his backpack.

But, as he headed out the door for second grade, he slowly turned back toward his mom with a curious look on his face and said, "Wait a minute, Mom. How do you get into the other kids' houses?"

***

Del-mar's Lab

Bubba said his cousin, Del-mar, who is Georgia-Tech-edumacated by the way, came to him and asked if he could set up a little lab building on Bubba and Tiny's farm. He promised he would stay out of their way and wouldn't do anything to hurt the chicken business.

Bubba talked it over with Tiny and they gave their permission. They figured whatever it was that Del-mar was wanting to do, it would be good for the world because after all, he had an engineering degree from Georgia Tech.

Well, they didn't pay much attention the first few weeks. Del-mar seemed to keep irregular hours. He'd come and go at all hours of the day and night. But, eventually curiosity got the best of them. One morning when they saw Del-mar enter the small building, they decided to go see for themselves what he was up to.

"What are you working on?" asked Tiny.

Del-mar grinned from ear to ear, "I'm trying to develop a universal solvent - something that will dissolve anything!"

Bubba piped up, "What good will that be?"

"Just imagine, Bubba... If we want a solution of gold, glass and iron... anything really... All we have to do is drop it in this solution," Del-mar beamed.

Tiny, as he was wont to do, threw a dose of reality on the situation, "That's nice, Del-mar. But, what are you gonna keep it in?"

In the cold light of day, Del-mar had to admit he hadn't considered this scientific quandary. The little shop was promptly closed up the next morning...

***

The Outhouse

Bubba said he and Bubba Sr were sitting on the front porch the other day just reminiscing. Bubba Sr brought up the 'outhouse incident.'

"You remember what happened with the outhouse?" asked Bubba Sr.

Bubba dropped his head a little but a sly grin crossed his face, "Yep. You called all us grandkids together and asked us who pushed over the outhouse."

"None of you kids spoke up so I told you the story of George Washington and how he cut down the cherry tree. His dad asked George if he did it and young George admitted as much," recounted Bubba Sr.

Bubba recalled, "You made a point of saying because George told the truth and fessed up, he didn't get a whipping. Then you asked us again, 'Who pushed over the outhouse?'"

"That's right," answered Bubba Sr.

Bubba said, "I remember telling you that you said George Washington told the truth and never got a whipping… boy, was I disappointed."

Bubba Sr replied, "Yes, but George Washington dad wasn't in the cherry tree when he chopped it down."

***

What's the Opposite?

When Bubba's cousin, Del-mar, attended Georgia Tech, the students in the psychology program had to attend a class on emotional extremes.

"Just to establish some parameters," said the professor to the student from Arkansas, "what is the opposite of joy?"

"Sadness," said the student.

"And the opposite of depression?" he asked of the young lady from Oklahoma.

"Elation," she said.

"And you sir," he said to the young man from Texas, "what about the opposite of woe?"

The Texan replied, "Sir, I believe that would be 'giddy up'"

***

The Essay
Suzie's teacher asked the class to write an essay on 'What they were thankful for on Thanksgiving.'

Later in the day, as the teacher collected the papers, she read with interest how some kids were thankful for all sorts of different things. That is until she got to Suzie's...

It had a single sentence on the page - 'I'm thankful I'm not a turkey.'

***

English Lesson
Suzie's school teacher wrote the following sentence on the blackboard, "I ain't had no fun all week." She turned to the class and asked, "How can I correct this sentence?"

A boy from the back of the class hollered, "Maybe you ought get a boyfriend."

***

Can't Help It
One of Suzie's little friends in Elementary School was called down by the teacher for talking in class. The teacher told him, "If you keep talking out of turn while I'm speaking I'm going to have to punish you. Do you understand?"

The boy replied, "I know teacher but I just can't help it. My dad is a preacher and my mom is a woman."

***

Failure Ain't Forever

Bubba and Tiny were talking about his college-educated cousin, Del-mar, the other day. Tiny, knowing all the trouble Del-mar's had during his life commented, "You know a lot of people don't think much of what Del-mar's done with his life."

Bubba replied, "Well, it ain't like he's been a failure. He just started on the bottom and he kind of likes it there..."

***

Chapter 7 - Why Do Banks Have Branches... If Money Doesn't Grow on Trees?

Once More for $20

Some folks may not be aware of this but Tiny and Bubba serve as co-presidents of the local Chicken Farmers Guild. This group gets together once a month over at Cracker Barrel to talk about the latest trends and news in the world of Poultry.

Tiny told me last month the speaker they had arranged to come talk to the group had cancelled at the last minute. He and Bubba were racking their brain, (Yes, I did say, 'Their brain', not 'brains') trying to figure out who they could get to come and speak.

In the meantime, two young men showed up at their door and offered to do some chores around the farm in exchange for a meal. Bubba put them to chopping wood out behind the house. Not ten minutes later, Tiny looked out the kitchen window to see one of the young men whirl across the barnyard, performing a succession of double flips and one-handed cartwheels before disappearing into the bushes.

Tiny ran outside, grabbed the second man by the arm and shouted, "That was amazing! Do you think your friend would be willing to do that again at the Chicken Farmers Guild this afternoon? I'll pay him twenty dollars!"

"Hey JoeDon," yelled the second young man. "This guy here wants to know if you'd chop off another finger for twenty bucks!"

***

Panhandling, Gainesville Style

Bubba's best blonde gal, Marg, has always been a soft touch according to Bubba. The other day she saw a panhandler at a busy intersection. She rolled down her car window and passed a dollar bill to the begging man.

Marg commented, "Poor man! Are you married?"

The begger replied--"Pardon me, madam! Do you think I'd be relyin' on total strangers for support if I had a wife?"

***

Government Benefits?

Bubba said his cousin, Junior, (Yep, the one that couldn't find a girlfriend his mom and dad could agree on), recently joined the local Army Reserve unit. You know they haven't done much fighting lately but they still are assigned certain jobs they have to perform. Junior was assigned to the Induction Center where he was to advise new recruits about their government benefits, especially their GI insurance.

After a couple of months his captain noticed that Junior had almost a 100 percent record for insurance sales - something that had never been achieved before.

Rather than ask him the secret of his success, the captain decided to stand at the back of the room and listen to Junior's sales pitch.

First, Junior explained the basics of the GI insurance to the new recruits, and then said:

"If you have GI insurance and go into battle and are killed, the government has to pay $200,000 to your beneficiaries. If you don't have GI insurance, and you go into battle and get killed, the government has to pay only a maximum of $6,000.

"Now," Junior concluded, "which bunch do you think they are going to send into battle first?"

Sold!

***

Be Sure to Take Advantage

Bubba said Uncle Fred and his wife, Evelyn, just got back from staying the weekend at a very exclusive resort. This place had everything - swimming pool, hair dryer in the bathroom, Pay TV in their bedroom, the works.

Well, when they got ready to check out, Fred went down to the desk to review the hotel bill. He noticed a couple of peculiar charges on the bill and asked the desk clerk about them.

"What's this fifty-dollar-a-day charge for fresh fruit? I didn't order any fresh fruit," Fred demanded.

The hotel clerk shot back, "It was in your room every day. It's not our fault if you didn't take advantage of it."

Fred grabbed the bill and subtracted $150 from the total. The hotel clerk asked Fred, "What do you think you're doing?"

"I'm deducting fifty-dollars-a-day for you kissing' my wife," Fred exclaimed.

"What? I didn't kiss your wife!" the clerk replied.

Fred smiled, "She was there every day. It ain't my fault you didn't take advantage of it."

***

Maternity Leave

Tiny's sister, Mavis Jean said she was working down at the local United Way, when her girlfriend, Maybelle, who is on maternity leave, brought her new bundle of joy to the office to show off to everyone.

She also had her seven-year-old son, Ace, with her. Everyone gathered around the baby, and the little boy asked, "Mommy, can I have some money to buy a Coke?"

"What do you say?" Maybelle asked.

Respectfully, Ace replied, "You're thin and beautiful."

Maybelle reached in her purse and gave her son the money.

***

Another Lawyer Joke

A local lawyer's wife died. At her funeral, the mourners were appalled to see that the headstone read: "Here lies Mary, wife of Spencer, L.L.D., Wills, Divorce, Malpractice, Personal Injury. Reasonable Rates."

Standing nearby, suddenly Spencer burst into tears.

His brother said: "You *should* be crying, pulling a disgraceful stunt like this!"

Spencer sobbed: "No, you don't understand. They left off the phone number!"

***

Jury Duty

Bubba's mom, Daisy, got called to serve on jury duty in Hall County recently. She told the court she wanted to be excused because she didn't believe in capital punishment and feared that her personal views might prevent the trial from running its proper course.

However, the prosecution lawyer liked Daisy's thoughtfulness and quiet assurance, and tried to convince her that she would make an excellent juror.

"Ma'm," he explained, "this is not murder trial! It's a simple civil lawsuit. A wife is bringing this case against her husband because he gambled away the $12,000 with which he had promised to buy her a new kitchen."

"Well, OK," agreed Daisy, her ears perking up upon hearing this explanation. "I'll serve. I guess I could be wrong about capital punishment after all."

***

Bank Robber

Tiny said he read in the local newspaper about a man who tried to rob the bank. Apparently according to an eyewitness, the man burst into the branch, ran up to a teller and yelled, "Give me all your money! Make one false move and you're geography!"

The teller corrected, "Don't you mean History?"

"Don't try to change the subject," the bank robber was reported to have replied.

The man in question is being held at the Hall County Detention Center.

***

Do Something Nice

Tiny said when his aunt Cledy's husband, Homer, died, one of her boys, Cletus, was unable to attend his dad's funeral because he lived so far away. (Cletus had moved to Alaska years ago to work in the oil fields.)

Anyway, he called his brother, Wade, and said, "Do something nice for Dad and send me the bill."

A few weeks later, he received a bill for $200, which he duly paid.

Then the next month he got another bill for $200, which he again paid, thinking it was some unforeseen expense.

But when the bills for $200 kept on arriving each month, Cletus phoned his brother, Wade, to find out what was going on.

"Well," said Wade, "you said to do something nice for Dad. So, I rented him a tuxedo."

***

What Would You Charge?

Boudreaux, Bubba's Louisiana brother-in-law, has always had a rascally sense of humor. He just can't resist putting one over on somebody. The other day while he was out mowing his yard, an attractive young lady in a Cadillac stopped in front of his house and motioned him over to her car.

Boudreaux sauntered over to the window and the young beauty said, "Mister, I just moved into this neighborhood and don't know a soul. What would you charge to come over and cut my grass?"

"Well, I don't rightly know, miss, but the lady what lives here lets me sleep with her."

***

Redneck Hotel?

Tiny said he has a surefire way to know if you're staying in a redneck hotel.

You call the front desk and say, "I've got a leak in the sink."

If the front desk person says, "Go ahead," yep, you're staying in a redneck hotel.

***

Delayed Honeymoon

Francine and some of the girls around the Highway Patrol office were talking about marriage one day. Francine told the gals, "Charles Thomas and I were married six months before we went on our honeymoon."

"Why'd you wait so long," asked one of the other female officers.

France replied, "We wanted to see how things would work out before we spent the money."

***

Ducking A Bet

Boudreaux and his friend, Enos, were out duck hunting a while back. They ended up making a bet on who could kill the most ducks with one bullet.

A flock of ducks flew over the bayou and Boudreaux let Enos have the first shot. He got nothing. A few minutes later another flock flew over and Boudreaux took a shot at them. Four ducks came tumbling down to earth.

"Pay up," said Boudreaux.

Enos shook his head, "I ain't a gonna do it. Them ducks would have died from the fall anyway."

***

Double or Nothin'

Tiny's uncle Merle was sitting at the breakfast table reading the stock market news. Aunt Lizzie was telling him how she'd tried all these different diet plans and they all had failed.

Merle looked up from the Morning Edition and said, "You know, you're the only investment I've ever made that's doubled."

***

The Sachet

Bubba's mom, Daisy, gave two of her young granddaughters a heart-shaped sachet for Valentine's Day. "You need to put that in your drawers so they will smell good," Daisy told the girls.

After smelling them for a while, the granddaughters asked Daisy, "Grandma, do we wear them in the front or in the back?"

***

Chapter 8 - Lick the Bowl - You Only Live Once

What's For Supper?

Boudreaux was watching television as his wife, Marie, was out cutting the grass during the hot summer. He went out to ask Marie what was for supper.

Well, Marie was quite irritated about Boudreaux sitting in the air conditioned house all day, looking at young babes in tight spandex, doing their exercises. Marie shot back at him, "Think of me as dead and do what you would do if I was."

Boudreaux went back into the house and fixed himself a big steak, baked potato, and a large glass of iced tea. Marie walked in about the time he was finishing up and asked, "So, you fixed something to eat? Where is mine?"

To which Boudreaux replied, "I thought you were dead..."

***

<u>Fish Tails</u>

Tiny said he and Bubba visited a coastal fishing village last summer. Considering themselves something of seafood connoisseurs, they stopped by a local restaurant for some lunch. Wanting to understand the general diet of the natives, Tiny asked the host, "What do most folks eat around here?"

The host replied, "Most folks eat fish of some sort everyday. It kind of goes with being close to the ocean."

Bubba protested, "But I thought fish is a brain food, and these folks are some of the most unintelligent-looking people that I ever saw."

"Mebbe so," the host agreed, trying to be polite. "But, just think what they'd look like if they didn't eat fish!"

***

The next day on that same trip, they spotted a sign in the window of a seafood restaurant that read, "Lobster Tails $2 each."

Sensing a bargain, they went inside and asked the waitress why they were so cheap. "They gotta be very short tails for that price," Bubba suggested.

"No," replied the waitress. "They're normal length."

Tiny countered, "Then they must be pretty old."

"No, they're fresh today," the waitress insisted.

"There's gotta be something wrong with them...," declared Bubba.

The waitress was emphatic, "No, they're just regular lobster tails."

"OK," said Tiny, "for two dollars we'll have one."

So, the waitress took their money, seated them at a table and said: "Once upon a time there was a big red lobster..."

***

Special Diet

Bubba said his cousin Junior told him his brother Earl (the one with the alligator pond down in Florida) had been having some personal problems of a delicate nature lately. Earl decided it was time to pay a visit to his doctor.

Earl told the the doc to do a full-on physical with all the blood and stool tests, etc. He was determined not to miss any tricks here. A few days later, the doctor had Earl come back in.

"I've come to the conclusion that you just need to eat more fiber, Earl. I'm starting you on a high-fiber diet today," said the doctor.

So, Earl left the office with a list of high-fiber foods he was supposed to eat. The list had beans and broccoli, berries, whole grains, dried fruits, apples, you name it - everything but the stuff Earl liked - pork chops, spare ribs, lots of butter.

Well, Earl stayed on this diet much to his dismay for the next two weeks. The doctor had scheduled a return appointment (as they as are inclined to do) and ran some more tests.

Again, Earl showed up back at the doc's to hear the verdict.

"I think we need to increase your fiber intake even more," proclaimed the doctor.

Earl shuttered, "Lord have mercy, Doc. I'm eatin' so much fiber now I passed a wicker basket the other day."

***

Cream and Sugar

Tiny said one of his farmer friend's, Pigeon Toe, lives out near the State Mental institution. The other day Pigeon Toe was driving his tractor pulling a wagon and happened to be going by said institution. One of the patients was standing out near the road and he asked Pigeon Toe, "What'd you got in the wagon?"

Pigeon Toe told him, "A load of manure."

"What you gonna do with it?" the patient inquired.

Pigeon calmly replied, "I'm gonna put it on my strawberries."

The patient shook his head and said, "I put cream and sugar on mine and they think I'm *crazy*!"

***

Juice Stand

Tiny said he and Bubba were driving down Interstate 75 the other day when a small sign indicated they had just crossed into Florida. A little further down the road they noticed a roadside stand that displayed a big sign advertising,

"Orange Juice. All you can drink for 25¢"

The boys were getting kind of thirsty so they pulled over at the stand and went up to the table.

Bubba plunked down a quarter and said, "I'll take you up on your juice deal!"

The attendant filled up a big glass with cool orange juice and handed it to Bubba. He quickly downed it and pushed the glass back for more, "Fill 'er up again!" he said.

The attendant did and said, "Okay. That'll be twenty-five cents, please."

"But, your sign says," Bubba started, "All you can drink for twenty-five cents."

The attendant looked at Bubba and said, "That *is* all you can drink for twenty-five cents."

***

The Dinner Party

Bubba said they had to get a new dog recently. It all started when they decided to have a dinner party and invite some guests. The menu consisted of salad and steaks with mushrooms. When it came time to cook, Bubba discovered he had no mushrooms.

"That's okay," said Tiny. "I'll go out in the woods and pick some wild ones."

"How will we know if they're poisonous?" asked Bubba.

Tiny said, "We'll feed some to the dog first."

The dog seemed to like the wild mushrooms and the dinner party was all going to plan. The guests arrived and ate heartily until one of them, Del-mar, came back into the dining room and announced he had witnessed the death of the family dog!

Well, Tiny and Bubba panicked and rushed their friends to the hospital to have their stomachs pumped. After the ordeal was over, Bubba asked Del-mar, "Did the dog have to suffer very long?"

"No," Del-mar replied. "That semi truck that hit him pretty much killed him instantly."

***

The Tootsie Pop

Bubba saw his cousin, Junior eating a Tootsie Roll Pop and asked him, "So, how many licks does it take to get to the center of a Tootsie Roll - Tootsie Pop?"

Without a thought, Junior replied, "Beats me, but it took almost the whole day just to lick through the wrapper."

***

Cheap Gas

Tiny reflected on the high price of fuel the other evening. He told Bubba he had paid $1.39 for gas earlier in the day.

Bubba asked, "$1.39? Where in the world did you find gas that cheap?"

"Taco Bell," replied Tiny.

***

Try the Chicken

Tiny said his Uncle Merle and Aunt Lizzie visited a very swanky buffet in downtown Gainesville the other evening. Merle apparently loved the chicken they were serving and kept going back repeatedly for more.

"That's the fifth time you've went back for chicken," Aunt Lizzie said as she leaned over to Merle. "Ain't you gettin' a little embarrassed?" Merle smiled, "Not at all. I keep tellin' 'em it's for my wife."

***

Chapter 9 - Dreaming of A World Where A Chicken Can Cross the Road Without His Motives Being Questioned

Chicken Suicide?

Bubba told me he had to call the Hall County Sheriff the other day after they had caught a feller trespassing on the chicken farm.

"Look here," said the commanding officer to the Bubba when they took the man down to the jail, "are you sure that this is the man who shot your chicken? Will you swear to it?"

"No, I won't do that," replied Bubba, "but I will say he's the man I suspect of doing it."

"That's not enough to convict somebody," retorted the county officer, considerably annoyed. "What raised your suspicions?"

"Well," replied Bubba, "It was like this--I saw him on my property with a gun; then I heard the gun go off; then I saw him putting the chicken in his knapsack; and it didn't seem to make sense to think the bird committed suicide."

***

Cooped Up

Tiny's old farmer friend down the road went into town to talk to the local air conditioning man. "I need to get an estimate on what it would cost to air condition my chicken coop," said the farmer. "I notice they tend to lay more eggs in the cool weather."

Ever the salesman, the air conditioning man asked, "While I'm out there would you like an estimate on the house too?"

"Nah, that's okay," said the farmer. "My wife don't lay eggs."

***

Load of Hay

Bubba said his preacher, Preacher Davis bought his little girl a pony recently. Not knowing much about the care of large farm animals but understanding they need lots of food, he ordered a load of hay from one of his parishioners. About noon on the agreed day of delivery, the parishioner's little son, Rusty, came to the house crying lustily.

On being asked what was the matter, Rusty wailed, "The load of hay tipped over in the street."

Preacher Davis, a kindly man, assured the little fellow that it was nothing serious and asked him in to dinner.

"Pa wouldn't like it," said Rusty.

But, Preacher Davis assured him, "Don't worry. I'll fix it all right with your dad. Stay and have some dinner before going back for the hay."

After dinner the boy was asked if he was glad that he had stayed.

"Pa ain't gonna like it," Rusty persisted.

Preacher Davis, unable to understand, asked the boy what made him think his dad would get mad.

"Pa's under the hay," said Rusty.

***

Pig Time

Improved farming technology makes its way slowly to some parts of North Georgia. Tiny said he was driving down the road the other day and seen a man feeding his pigs. He stopped and watched as the farmer would lift a pig up to a nearby apple tree allowing the pig to eat the apples off the tree. The farmer moved the pig from one apple to another until the pig was satisfied. Then he'd grab another pig and start the whole process over again.

Tiny watched with astonishment for a while until he couldn't resist. He walked up to the farmer and said, "Just think of the time you'd save if you shook them apples off of the tree and let the pigs eat them off the ground."

The farmer had a puzzled look on his face and asked, "What's time to a pig?"

***

Hay Business

Bubba's cousins from opposite sides of the family, Del-mar and Junior, went into business recently. They are selling bails of hay. They buy a truck load of it at one price, haul it and sell it for less than they paid.

After a week of this, Del-mar, who is college-educated by-the-way, told Junior, "We've got to do something about this hay business. We are not making any money! We're buying it for one price and selling it for a lower price!"

Junior, who does not have the benefit of a college education, told his partner after some thought on the matter, "I guess we're just gonna have to get us a bigger truck."

***

Never Been to Kentucky

Bubba said one of the old farmers down the road noticed a jogger running down his country road the other morning. The farmer wasn't surprised when he heard his horse yell to the jogger, "Hey, buddy - come over here."
He watched with interest as the jogger slowed, came over to his horse standing near the fence and stopped.

The jogger asked, "Were you talking to me?"

The horse replied, "Sure was. Man, I've got a problem. I won the Kentucky Derby a few years ago and this farmer bought me and now all I do is pull a plow and I'm sick of it. Why don't you run up to the house and offer him $5,000 to buy me. I'll make you some big money 'cause I can still run."

The jogger thought to himself, 'boy, a talking horse.' Dollar signs started appearing in his head.

The old farmer was sitting on the porch as the jogger approached. He grinned to himself as the jogger came up the hill.

The jogger told the farmer, "Hey, I'll give you $5,000 for that old broken down nag you've got in the field."

The farmer replied, "Son, you can't believe anything that horse says - He's never even been to Kentucky."

***

BTU's Explained

Bubba said one of the old farmer's down the road was complaining his air conditioner had gone out. The lack of air conditioning was making his wife particularly irritating to live with. Bubba told him the hardware store was running a big sale and he ought to go check it out.

The salesman walked over as the farmer entered the hardware store, "Can I help you?"

'Yes, I'm looking for an air conditioner," replied the farmer.

The salesman pulled him over and started showing him one of their products. "I've got this 12,000 BTU unit on sale. It's a dandy."

The farmer studied the unit. Meantime, the salesman tugged on his coat and pulled him toward an even larger air conditioner. "This 15,000 BTU unit is also on sale."

The old farmer looked it over. The salesman pulled him toward another unit and started, "I've also got this 18,000 BTU..."

The farmer cut him off in mid-sentence, "Listen I don't understand nothin' about these BTU's. I just want an air conditioner big enough to cool a B.U.T. as big as a T.U.B."

***

Pen or Pencil?

Bubba was reading the Gainesville Times recently which carried an article about how when NASA first started sending up astronauts, they quickly discovered that ball-point pens would not work in zero gravity.

He read the newspaper to Tiny, "To combat this problem, NASA scientists spent a decade and $12 billion developing a pen that writes in zero gravity, upside down, underwater, on almost any surface including glass and at temperatures ranging from below freezing to over 300° F."

Tiny characteristically replied, "Why couldn't they have just used a pencil? Been a whole lot cheaper..."

***

Life Expectancy

Bubba said his cousin, Junior, visited the doctor's office last week. Junior is about as straight an arrow as you can get when it comes to taking care of his health. You might even say he's risk-averse; he wouldn't cross the road if his mailbox wasn't on the other side. Anyway, always vigilent about his fitness, Junior asked Doc White, "Do you think I shall live until I'm ninety, doctor?"

"How old are you now?" replied Doc White.

"Forty."

Doc White inquired, "Do you drink, gamble, smoke, or have you any vices of any kind?"

"No. I don't drink, I never gamble, I loathe smoking; in fact, I don't have any vices," Junior responded with a proud grin.

Doc White frowned, "Well, good heavens, what in the world do you want to live another fifty years for?"

***

And, speaking of doctors, Junior told Bubba he overheard two of them whispering in the hall when he was over at the Hall County clinic.

"Well," said the first doctor, "What's new this morning?"

The second doc rubbed his chin as he spoke, "I've got a most curious case. Woman, cross-eyed; in fact, so cross-eyed that when she cries the tears run down her back."

"What are you doing for her?" asked the first doc.

The second doctor spoke up, "Just now we've started treating her for bacteria."

***

Lazy Farmer

Bubba said one of the laziest farmers he's ever met lives just down the road from him. The other day he and Tiny drove by this man's farm and noticed his barn was on fire.

"Clyde, your barn's burning down!" Bubba hollered.

The lazy farmer replied, "I know. I'm sittin' here prayin' for rain."

***

Farm Marriage

Bubba said he talked to a farmer up the road the other day and the feller told him he'd been married 49 years. Bubba asked him what the secret was to living with somebody that long on a farm.

"Well," the farmer started, "We get along pretty good. When it's harvest time and she's out in the field, she can pull corn and act like a scarecrow all at the same time."

***

Hen or Rooster?

Tiny said when Mavis Jean's kids were young they took them to Cracker Barrel for dinner one day. Her boy, Troy Allen, couldn't have been more than five at the time.

Trying to prove he was a big boy, Troy Allen left the table to go to the bathroom by himself. A few minutes later he returned with a confused look on his face. "Mama, am I a Hen or a Rooster?"

***

Absent Minded

Tiny drove past one of his farmer friends the other day. This man was known to be a little absent minded. He stood there on the side of the road holding a bridle.

Tiny asked, "What you got there, Jerry?"

Perplexed, Jerry said, "I'm not sure if I found a bridle or lost a horse."

***

Chapter 10 - May Contain Alcohol

Really Livin'

Tiny and Bubba just got back from taking a business trip up north. They visited Milwaukee with several other country farmers. Seems one of the big Midwestern seed companies was sponsoring a convention up there.

While attending this meeting, the convention hosts arranged for a tour of one of the big beer breweries in town. The guests ambled from room to room seeing giants vats of hops, water and beer. One of their party happened to be standing over a large vat of beer, when he slipped and fell in, drowning in the process.

Tiny and Bubba were tasked with telling his wife what had happened when they got back to Gainesville. They took Bubba's Uncle Fred along for moral support since he had known the older gentleman.

"Did he suffer much before he died?," asked the wife.

Tiny put his hand on the woman's shoulder, "No. In fact, he climbed out three times to use the restroom before he drowned!"

Fred, who loves to tip a jug, just shook his head, "Man, that's really livin'."

***

A Huntin' We Will Go

Bubba's cousin, Del-mar, was down at the Hall County Sheriff's Office the other day explaining why his friend, BillyBob, had shot him.

"We wuz havin' us a real good time drinkin'," Del-mar explained, "when my friend, Billy Bob, picked up his rifle and asked us fellas if we wanna go a huntin'."

"Okay, then what happened?" the officer asked.

"That's when I stood up and said, 'Sure. I'm game!'"

***

The Wisdom of Fred

Bubba's Uncle Fred, who was known to tug on a cork or two, had a favorite saying, "Liquor kills more people than bullets. But, I'd rather be full of Liquor than full of bullets."

Uncle Fred did have a solid cure for hangover's though - Keep drinking.

Known for his concern for his fellow man, Fred would tell the boys down at the local watering hole, "Be sure to always use a bottle opener. Otherwise, you'll ruin your gums."

***

Shirt Pocket

Bubba told me his Aunt Evelyn had called him the other day. It seems Uncle Fred had stopped by his favorite watering hole and had not come back home. Evelyn asked if Bubba would go down and fetch him. She didn't want him getting another ticket from the Police.

Bubba arrived and saw Fred bellied up at the bar. He noticed a man next to Fred who ordered a shot of whiskey and a beer. The man drank the shot, chased it with the beer and then looked into his shirt pocket.

This continued several times before Bubba's curiosity got the best of him. He leaned over to the guy next to Uncle Fred and said, "'Cuse me, I couldn't help but notice your little ritual, why in the world do you look into your shirt pocket every time you drink your whiskey and beer?"

The man replied, "There's a picture of my wife in there, and when she starts lookin' good, I'm headin' home!"

Bubba collected Fred and brought him on to the house.

***

Typical Politician

Bubba Sr went to a local political rally last week. Wanting to speak with his elected official, he waited until most of the crowd had left before approaching the Congressman.

Being a preacher, Bubba Sr asked about his attitude toward whiskey.

The Congressman spouted, "If you mean the demon drink that poisons the mind, pollutes the body, desecrates family life, and inflames sinners, then I'm against it."

"But if you mean the elixir of Christmas cheer, the shield against winter chill, the taxable potion that puts needed funds into public coffers to comfort little crippled children, then I'm for it."

"This is my position, and I will not compromise!"

Bubba Sr. said he left the gathering not knowing any more than when he came.

***

One More Time

Bubba's Aunt Evelyn had just about had it with Uncle Fred coming home drunk every night. She told him, "If you come home drunk one more time, I'll turn you into a rat!"

Well, the next night you can guess what happened. As a soused Fred approached the front door of his house with a friend, Fred told the fella as he pointed toward the porch, "If you suddenly see me getting smaller and smaller, keep your eye on that cat!"

***

Drinking is Bad for Your Health

Bubba said his Uncle Fred had read recently that drinking was bad for his health. Bubba asked him, "What did you do?"

Fred said, "I quit reading."

If that wasn't bad enough Aunt Evelyn told him he was spending too much money on alcohol and that he needed to quit. Amazingly, he did.

Fred said he noticed the next week Evelyn spent $65 on make-up. He asked her, "Why in the world are you spending all that money on make-up?"

Aunt Evelyn answered, "I'm doing it for you so you'll think I look pretty."

Fred replied, "Why do you think I was doing all that drinking..."

***

Pet Rat

Uncle Fred was telling Bubba how he used to own a pet rat. Fred had taught this rat how to talk and also how to drink liquor. Whenever he went out he would carry the rat in his coat pocket. One day Fred went into a bar and took the rat with him.

Fred ordered two drinks. He drank the first one and slowly poured the second one into his coat pocket. The bartender, seeing this strange behavior, decided not to let Fred have any more to drink.

When Fred ordered two more drinks, the bartender said, "I'm sorry, fella. You've already had enough."

"I've only had one drink," Fred protested. "Let me see the manager! Get him out here!"

Just then the rat stuck his head up out of Fred's coat pocket and said, "Yeah! And tell him to bring his stupid cat with him too!"

***

The Eyes Have It

Tiny's Texas Highway Patrol cousin, Francine, pulled a man over for speeding last week and asked him to get out of the car. After looking the man over Francine asked, "Sir, I can't help but notice your eyes are bloodshot. Have you been drinking?"

The man got real indignant with her and said, "Officer, I can't help but notice your eyes are glazed. Have you been eating doughnuts?"

***

Visit to the Cemetery

Bubba said his Uncle Fred visited a friend of his the other day - in the cemetery. Fred placed a bottle of beer on the man's headstone and stepped back for a moment of silence. Nearby was one of the busybodies from 3rd Baptist placing some flowers on a grave.

Thinking it a strange form of memorial, she piped up, "When exactly do you expect your friend to come up and drink the beer?"

Uncle Fred smiled, "The same time your friend comes up to smell the flowers."

***

The Cure is Worse Than the Bite

Aunt Evelyn called the other day to tell Bubba that her husband, Fred, had developed a bad habit of chewing his fingernails. She had tried everything she could think of but nothing seemed to work.

Bubba told her, "Leave him with me a couple of days and I'm pretty sure I can cure him."

True to his word, Bubba drove Uncle Fred back home a couple days later and proclaimed him cured.

"What in the world did you do to get him to stop chewing his nails?" asked Evelyn.

Bubba smiled, "We took his teeth away from him."

***

Grandfather Clock

Bubba Sr went to one of the local auction houses last Friday night and ended up buying himself a grandfather clock. Feeling good about his purchase, he decided to carry it home. He hadn't got a hundred feet down the street before a drunk bumped into him and caused him to drop the clock.

"Why don't you watch where you're going? Look what you've done!" exclaimed Bubba Sr.

The drunk, nonplussed, responded, "Why don't you wear a wristwatch like everybody else?"

***

Drunk Haircut

Speaking of Fred, Bubba said he wandered into the barbershop the other day, drunk as a monkey. He had his hat pulled down over his ears as he shouted, "Gimme a haircut."

"You'll have to take your hat off," the barber replied.

Fred dutifully pulled the cap off, "Oh excuse me. I didn't know there were ladies present."

***

Out the Window

Fred actually fell out of a two story window one day; He was so drunk. When he regained consciousness, a big crowd was gathered around him. A Gainesville policeman asked Fred, "What happened?"

Fred said, "I don't know. I just got here."

***

Chapter 11 - Lawyers, Serial Killers and Other Professionals

Jury Duty

Bubba told me his grandpa, Bubba Sr, got a letter in the mail notifying him he had been selected for jury duty in Gainesville. He was a bit surprised so he called the clerk's office to remind them that he was exempt because of his age.

"You need to come in and fill out the exemption forms," the clerk said.

Bubba Sr protested, "I did that last year."

"You have to do it every year," the clerk insisted.

Bubba Sr replied, "Why? Do you think I'm going to get younger?"

***

Knowing the Future

Tiny said he was talking to cousin Francine's father-in-law, Herschel, about death and the future. The point Tiny was trying to make was that no one knows the *when*, *where* or *how* of their own death.

Herschel piped up, "My brother, Hiram, did. He knew the very day, the hour, even the *how* of when he was going to die."

"How in the world could he know those things, Herschel?" answered Tiny.

Herschel didn't miss a beat, "Because the judge told him."

***

It's Okay. He's Single

Bubba Sr was telling about two of his female friends that live over in Lanier Village, the housing development designed just for seniors (old folks). These two widow ladies named Rhoda and Dennie were curious about the new gentleman who moved in down the hall from them. He was quiet and distinguished and seemed to be keeping to himself.

One day Rhoda said to Dennie, "You know how I am in matters like this. You are much more confident. Why don't you ambush him at the pool and find out a little more about him. He looks so lonely."

So, Dennie went over to talk to the man as he sat by the pool. "My friend and I were wondering why you look so lonely," she said.

"Of course I'm lonely," the man snapped. "I've spent the last 30 years in prison."

Dennie pried a little more, "Oh, really. Why?"

"I strangled my third wife," replied the man.

"Oh, really. What happened to your second wife?" Dennie wondered.

The man retorted, "We had a fight and she fell off a tall building."

"Oh, my."

Dennie turned to her friend who was on the other side of the pool and hollered, "Yoo-hoo, Rhoda! It's okay. He's single."

***

Cure for Burglars

Tiny told me his Uncle Merle was going to bed the other night when his wife, Tizzie, told him that he'd left the light on in the shed. Merle opened the backdoor to go out and turn off the light but saw there were people in the shed in the process of stealing his things.

Merle immediately called the police, who asked "Is someone in your house?"

Merle replied, "No, they are in my shed out back."

The officer on duty explained, "All our patrols are busy. Just lock your door and an officer will be there later when available."

Merle said, "Okay," hung up, counted to 30, and phoned the police again.

"Hey, I just called you a few seconds ago because there were people in my shed. Well, you don't have to worry about them now because I've just shot all of them."

Then Merle hung up.

Within five minutes three squad cars, an Armed Response unit, and an ambulance showed up. Of course, the police caught the burglars red-handed.

One of the police officer's said to Merle: "I thought you said that you'd shot them!"

Merle said, "I thought you said there was nobody available!"

***

The Psychiatrist

It's a given that Bubba's dad and mom, Lum and Daisy, aren't necessarily the sharpest tools in the shed. I'm not saying they are crazy or anything but Daisy did take Lum to a local shrink last week.

"I've got to do something about Lum, Doctor. He thinks he's a refrigerator," explained Daisy.

The Psychiatrist examined Lum and came out to talk with Daisy afterwards. "Daisy, you don't have anything to worry about. I think Lum will get over all this business of thinking he's a refrigerator."

"Oh, I know that, Doc. But, he sleeps with his mouth open and that little old light keeps me awake all night."

***

Doctor's Orders

And speaking of visiting the doctor, one of Tiny's farmer friends went to see their local family physician. After a very thorough examination the doctor told the older gentleman he didn't have long to live.

"What do you recommend I do with the time I have left, Doc?" asked the old farmer.

The Doctor scratched his head and replied, "You need to go buy you an old worn-out station wagon, find the ugliest and meanest woman you can with six or seven kids, marry her and all of you take a road trip to Mexico."

"How will that make me live longer, Doc?" asked the man.

"I didn't say it would make you live longer but it will sure *seem* like you have."

***

New Policy

Smoking has fallen out of favor these past few years. Many stores have adopted a 'No Smoking' policy. Bubba said he was in a drugstore the other day that had enacted just such a rule. Shortly, a man walked in enjoying a smoke.

"Sir, I'm sorry but you'll have to put out your cigarette," said the clerk.

The customer responded a little indignant, "Well, you sell them in this store don't you?"

"Yes," the clerk countered. "We also sell Ex-Lax but you don't see anyone in here enjoying it, do you?"

***

Ice Fishing

Bubba's friends, BillyBob, BillyRay and BillyJoe went ice fishing awhile back when we had that real cold spell. There was only room for two of them upfront in the truck cab once they got all their fishing gear inside.

"Looks like you're gonna need to ride in the bed of the truck, BillyJoe," said BillyBob.

They drove out on the lake to a spot where they thought the ice had frozen good and solid. Wrong! The truck broke through the ice and immediately sank to the bottom. BillyBob and BillyRay quickly opened the windows of the pickup and swam up to the hole the truck made in the ice. Shivering, they crawled out and waited for BillyJoe who had been riding in the back.

Minutes seemed like minutes as they waited for their friend to appear. After a long delay, BillyJoe finally popped up to the surface. The two friends were surprised that he was under for so long and asked, "What took you so long?"

"Well, I had some trouble," BillyJoe answered. "I couldn't get the tailgate down."

***

Speaking of Funerals

Wade, Cledy's boy, told Tiny he was out at his dad's grave the other day when he saw a smartly dressed woman march into the cemetery and confront a funeral director.

"I've looked all over the cemetery," she raged, "and I can't find my husband's grave or head stone anywhere."

"What name is it, please?" asked the director.

"Alec Wildenstein."

The director searched through his files. "Hmm," he said. "There must be some mistake. All we have here is a Gloria Wildenstein."

"No mistake," said the annoyed woman. "That's my husband, all right. Everything is in my name."

***

Same 'Ole, Same 'Ole

Tiny said his uncle and aunt, Merle and Tizzie, had been revisiting Merle's hometown recently. He hadn't been back there in forty years. They enjoyed their trip so much they decided to go again this year. They visited the same shops, parks, restaurants and stayed in the same hotel they had previously. Tizzie even got her hair done at the same hairdressers.

When she went to the beauty salon, the owner asked Tizzie if she was from around there. "You look familiar. Have you been here before?" the owner inquired.

"Actually, I have. It's been a year since you did my hair," answered Tizzie.

Upon hearing this, one of the elderly ladies in the shop piped up, "Well, I'll be, honey. It sure did keep good."

***

Pumping Sewage

Tiny said before he passed last year, his aunt Cledy's husband, Homer, was telling him about being stationed at Thule Air Base in Greenland during the war. A cargo plane was preparing for departure and they were waiting for the truck to arrive to pump out the aircraft's sewage tank.

The aircraft commander was becoming impatient. Not only was the truck late, but also the airman performing the job, in this case, Homer, was extremely slow in getting the tank pumped out.

Finally the commander snapped and promised

to punish Homer for his slowness.

Homer replied, "Sir, I have no stripes, it is twenty below zero, I'm stationed in Greenland, and I am pumping sewage out of airplanes. Just what are you going to do to punish me?"

The aircraft commander had to admit Homer had a point...

***

The Republican

Bubba said a Republican running for Congress stopped by his cousin Junior's brother Earl's farm last week. Earl, who lives in Florida is a staunch Democrat. Where he lives there ain't many Republicans who come around. When Earl heard this man was a Republican, he told the fella to wait right there just a minute. He wanted to go and get his ma; She'd never seen a Republican before.

The politician looked around for an appropriate platform from which to make a short speech. Finding nothing, he climbed up on a small mound of dried horse manure over near the side of the barn.

Earl came back shortly with his ma and the candidate waxed eloquent for a few moments. As he finished, Earl said, "That's the first time I've ever heard a Republican speak."

The politician said, "That's the first time I've ever given a Republican speech from a Democratic platform."

***

Just My Luck

Bubba said he talked to one of his Gainesville High School friends last week. He asked him, "Rayburn, it's been twenty years since we've seen each other. How's your wife doin'?"

Rayburn said, "Well, she ran off with a vacuum cleaner salesman ten years ago."

"That's too bad," Bubba replied awkwardly. "Well, how's your daughter doin'?"

"She was so upset about her mom that she wound up in a mental institution," answered Rayburn.

Bubba responded, "That's too bad. Well, how's your son doin'?"

"He was so upset about his mother that he went after the vacuum cleaner salesman and now he's serving a life sentence," replied Rayburn.

Stunned, Bubba was at a loss for words. "Well, what are you doin' now?"

"Oh, you know, the same 'ol' thing," said Rayburn. "Still selling good luck charms."

***

Court Appearance

Uncle Fred had been down at the local bar getting soused. When he came outside and got into his car, a police officer nabbed him and took him to the Hall County jail.

The next morning as Fred went to court, the judge said, "I thought I told you I never wanted to see you in here again."

Fred replied, "Your Honor, that's what I tried to tell the police, but they wouldn't listen."

***

Dead Owner?

Cousin Junior's friend, Dale, got arrested for stealing a car recently. His case came up and he stood before the judge. The judge asked him why he stole the vehicle since this was his first offense.

"Your honor, I didn't steal the car," replied Dale. "It was parked in front of a cemetery. I thought the owner was dead."

***

POSTSCRIPT

We've come to a place of repose in Tiny and Bubba's latest adventures. A literary bench as it were to sit down, kick our shoes off and take it easy for a few minutes. Their good fortunes continue as they look expectantly toward the future. Where will they go next? To the Fair? On vacation? To the Moon? It's un-telling!

One thing they really wanted me to communicate on their behalf is just how much they appreciate you, dear reader, coming along on the journey with them. What's the fun in taking a trip if there's nobody to share it with?

This is their third book of misadventures. Bubba said it was unbelievable that they had a trinity (I think he meant a 'trilogy') of books out. If you haven't read *The Life and Times of Tiny and Bubba: With Collected Wisdom Along the Way* OR *Tiny and Bubba: Back Down on the Farm*, they strongly encourage you to do so.

As their humble scribe, I am thrilled to hear so many people say, 'That book really made me laugh!' For without laughter, what's the point of it all anyway?

I hope one day we'll meet and you'll be able to say with so many others, 'That book made me laugh... or at least crack a smile...'

This page left intentionally blank. Draw a picture. Write a poem. Copy down the lyrics to a song you like.... The possibilities are endless...